Developing
POETRY SKILLS

Reading
Poetry
11–14

Geoff Barton

Heinemann Educational Publishers
Halley Court, Jordan Hill, Oxford OX2 8EJ
a division of Reed Educational and Professional Publishing Ltd

OXFORD BLANTYRE CHICAGO PORTSMOUTH NH (USA)
MELBOURNE AUCKLAND IBADAN GABORONE
JOHANNESBURG

First published 1998
02 01
10 9 8 7
ISBN 0 435 10412 8

Designed and produced by Gecko Ltd, Bicester, Oxon
Cover design by Gecko Ltd, Bicester, Oxon
Illustrations by Andrew Quelch, Gary Wing, Pantelis Palios and Tracy Rich
Printed and bound in Spain by Edelvives

Acknowledgements
The author and publishers wish to thank the following who have kindly granted permission for the use of copyright material: Random House UK Ltd for 'You Being Born' by Brian Jones, p14, from *Spitfire on the Northern Line* (Bodley Head Ltd); 'Stopping by Woods on a Snowy Evening' by Robert Frost, p28, from *The Poetry of Robert Frost* edited by Edward Connery Lathem (Jonathan Cape Ltd); 'Lone Dog' by Irene Rutherford McLeod, p48, from *Songs to Save a Soul* (Chatto & Windus Ltd) and 'An Ordinary Day' by Norman MacCaig, p82, from *Collected Poems*. Anvil Press Poetry Ltd for 'In Mrs Tilscher's Class' by Carol Ann Duffy, p16, from *The Other Country*, and 'Fable'; by Janos Pilinszky, p96, from *The Desert of Love: Selected Poems*, translated by Ted Hughes and Janos Csokits. Faber and Faber Ltd. for 'My Parents Kept Me from Children who were Rough' by Stephen Spender, p18, from *Collected Poems: 1928–1985;* 'Pompeii' by Judith Nicholls, p32, from *Magic Mirror;* 'To the Sea' by Philip Larkin, p36, from *High Windows;* 'Night Mail' by W. H. Auden, p64, from *Collected Poems: 1927–1957;* 'Death of a Naturalist' by Seamus Heaney, p97, from *New Selected Poems: 1966–1987;* 'Full Moon and Little Frieda' by Ted Hughes, p102, and 'Stop all the Clocks, cut off the Telephone' Twelve Songs IX by W. H. Auden, p108, from *Collected Poems*. Peterloo Poets for 'Small Incident in Library' by David Sutton, p20, from *Flints*. Headland Publications for 'The Minnow Catching Boys' by Susan Skinner, p22, from *The Minnow Catching Boys*. Laura Cecil on behalf of the James Reeves Estate for 'The Toadstool Wood', p26, and 'The Sea', p78, from *Complete Poems for Children* by James Reeves (Heinemann). Carcanet Press Ltd. for 'Hyena' by Edwin Morgan, p38, from *Collected Poems*. The Peters, Fraser & Dunlop Group Ltd on behalf of Laurie Lee for 'Town Owl', p40, from *Selected Poems* (Penguin Books); on behalf of the Estate of Hilaire Belloc for 'Tarantella', p70, from *Complete Verse* (Random House UK Ltd); on behalf of Roger McGough for 'The Lake', p88, from *Holiday on Death Row* (Jonathan Cape Ltd), 'Rabbit in Mixer Survives', p112, from *Selected Poems* (Penguin Books), and 'Being-in-love', p108; and on behalf of Walter Lord for an extract from *A Night to Remember,* p117. International Music Publications for 'The Lion and Albert', words by George Marriott Edgar, p42, © 1933 Francis Day & Hunter, London WC2H 0EA. Macmillan Publishers Ltd. on behalf of the Estate of Thomas Hardy for 'The Fallow Deer at the Lonely House', p44 and 'The Convergence of the Twain', p119, from *The Complete Poems of Thomas Hardy* edited by James Gibson (Papermac). James Kirkup for 'The Haunted Lift', p50. Hippopotamus Press for 'Prince Kano' by Edward Lowbury, p52, from *Collected Poems*. HarperCollins Publishers on behalf of the Estate of J. R. R. Tolkien for 'Far Over the Misty Mountains', p54, from *The Hobbit*. The Orion Publishing Group Ltd for 'The Survivors' by R. S. Thomas, p56, from *Collected Poems* (J. M. Dent). A. P. Watt Ltd on behalf of The National Trust for 'The Way Through the Woods' by Rudyard Kipling, p58. The Society of Authors representing the Literary Trustees of Walter de la Mare for 'The Listeners', p60, from *The Complete Poems of Walter de la Mare*. David Higham Associates Ltd. on behalf of Louis MacNeice for 'Prayer Before Birth', p66, from *Collected Poems of Louis MacNeice* (Faber and Faber), and on behalf of Elizabeth Jennings for 'The Smell of Chrysanthemums', p106, from *Collected Poems* (Carcanet Press). Little Brown & Company (UK) for 'Woman Work' by Maya Angelou, p68, from *And Still I Rise* (Virago Press). Oxford University Press for 'A Martian Sends a Postcard Home' by Craig Raine, p74, from *A Martian Sends a Postcard Home*; 'In the Nursery' by Anne Stevenson, p80, from *Collected Poems of Anne Stevenson: 1955–1995*, and 'For a Five-Year-Old' by Fleur Adcock, p100, from *Selected Poems*. Vernon Scannell for 'A Case of Murder', p86. Gerald Duckworth & Company for an extract from *Every Man for Himself* by Beryl Bainbridge, p118.

Whist every effort has been made to locate the owners of copyright, in some cases this has been unsuccessful. The publishers apologise for any omission of original sources and will be pleased to make the necessary arrangements at the first opportunity.

The Publishers would also like to thank the following for permission to reproduce photographs on the pages noted: Hulton Getty pp18, 24, 34, 36–7; Images p28; Corbis p32; Imagebank pp68, 78–9; FLPA pp93, 112, 115.

Contents

Introduction

Skills *and* knowledge

Developing Poetry Skills 11–14 is a poetry book to meet the varied needs of the whole of Key Stage 3. It aims to provide students with a poetry foundation that will prepare them for the syllabus demands of Key Stage 4.

The book is distinctive because it explicitly develops students' skills in reading poetry. Too often we treat poetry like any other text. We read it, discuss it and then perhaps write about it. But we don't always gnaw away at the distinctiveness of poetry – at what makes a poem a poem.

This book gets students reading poetry actively and critically and – from the start of Year 7 – analysing, debating and interrogating the poems they read. Written against a background of increasingly urgent attention to literacy, *Developing Poetry Skills 11–14* has high expectations of what pupils can achieve through rigorous, step-by-step activities. Some of my best Year 7 lessons have been spent untangling poems which I might have read with Year 12 students. A colleague of mine makes a speciality of teaching Milton to Year 8. We've all seen how Shakespeare, well taught, can excite Year 9 students.

Of course, reading poetry involves many of the literacy skills used in reading other types of texts. These 'foundation skills' are emphasised throughout this book. But to become a sensitive and more subtle reader of poetry, students also need to develop more specialised skills and areas of understanding. This book aims to teach these more systematically. The purpose? Not to create students who can quack the appropriate technical term or spot enjambment at three metres, but rather to enhance the quality of students' responses to poetry.

The book has been compiled in that spirit – with the notion that carefully structured poetry activities and an introduction to critical terms can build students' confidence and enhance their response to poetry.

The list of poetry skills covered in the book is provided on page 8, and these skills are cross-referenced against individual poems, so that you can ensure coverage of texts and activities that best suits your students.

Structure

The book starts with a thematic approach. The first three units are ideal for Year 7. Then the focus shifts to language and structure appropriate for Year 8. By Year 9, students are introduced to genres and prepared for the comparative requirements they will face at GCSE.

Developing Poetry Skills 11–14 contains the work of many of the poets required for National Curriculum coverage, with a core of accessible pre-1900 texts and a range of poetic genres. The book therefore leads students through a structured sequence, giving them a broad base of activities and skills to prepare them, finally, for their GCSE course. If Key Stage 3 creates the breadth students need, they will then have the skills to tackle individual poets in depth at GCSE.

Differentiation

The book is aimed at the range of students who will be sitting Key Stage 3 tests at the end of Year 9. It allows for a number of approaches to differentiation, as follows.

- The book as a whole is sequential: initial units are more immediately accessible than later ones. Bear in mind that units 1–3 are notionally targeted at Year 7; units 4–6 at Year 8; and 7–9 at Year 9.

- Within each unit, texts and activities are progressive. Students can be led from one to the next, building confidence as they go. In some classrooms groups of students within the same class may be working at different levels and on different poems; or, if on the same poem, some may work on the earlier tasks while another group is set a more demanding one.

- Support for all students is provided in the form of clear layout, illustrations to reinforce meanings, language panels to teach key terms explicitly, a glossary to allow easy reference, and a final close reading task so that you can – if you wish – assess students in formal conditions to monitor their progress.

Using the book

Developing Poetry Skills 11–14 provides a range of activities, just like its companion book, *The Real World: Media and Non-Fiction 11–14*. Students use discussion, writing, analysis and comprehension to explore texts. Occasionally they use drama and IT, but in general this is a book about developing close reading skills, and the activities therefore keep probing the language and structure of texts rather than leading students on to a wider level of response.

Each unit starts with a brief starting point and then features usually a double-page spread of a poem plus activities. Each unit ends with a close reading exercise: a single poem, plus questions, to sharpen students' ability to respond to the detail of poetry.

We have also included a series of assignments at the end of the book. These are broader tasks, based on the reading within each unit but taking students into other coursework possibilities. The assignments have been structured so that the first one relating to a given unit is the more accessible, the later one the more demanding.

Analysing poetry

I believe that technical terms can actually sharpen students' responses to texts (once you know the term alliteration, you spot the effect more easily), and I never shy away from teaching technical terms with my students. I wouldn't avoid using photosynthesis in biology, so why avoid stanza or lyric when teaching poetry? In my experience, students are flattered to be taught the terms and quickly begin to apply them for themselves.

For this reason, activities lead students into far greater depth of analysis than we might ever have dared to expect a few years ago. The emphasis is on getting them to grapple with poems actively, exploring the language for themselves. I have assumed throughout that students will frequently work on the tasks in groups, and through discussion rather than writing, so I have rarely prescribed groupings or spoken/written work. Similarly, I have started and ended with the assumption that personal response comes first – but that it grows out of sound understanding and close attention to language. This leads to *informed* personal response rather than mere gut reaction.

The book will be most effective when different poems are studied over a number of lessons, rather than as isolated one-offs. This will help to build confidence, allow analytical skills to be developed by applying them to a range of texts, and deepen students' responses to poetry by letting them hear different rhythms and see different structures. These are important foundations that we are building.

Conclusion

I hope you can sense the enthusiasm I have for this collection. Putting it together was a marvellous opportunity – old classroom favourites brought together with new finds, all combined in a package that is designed to make a significant impact on the student's ability to respond to poetry.

I hope you will enjoy using it.

Geoff Barton

Poetry skills	Main focus
1 Understanding the main **ideas** in the poem	*particular emphasis in units 1–3 (using comprehension-style questions); then throughout*
2 Being able to comment on the **narrator's voice**	*unit 1*
3 Making comments about the **purpose** and **audience**	*unit 1*
4 Learning to discuss **imagery** – use of simile, metaphor and personification	*unit 1* *unit 2*
Noticing the way the writer uses **sounds** – patterns, echoes, onomatopoeia	*unit 2* *unit 3* *unit 5*
6 Exploring the writer's use of **vocabulary** – word associations, senses, cliché, word origins, poetry versus prose	*unit 2* *unit 3* *unit 4* *unit 5*
7 Commenting with confidence upon the writer's use of **rhythm**	*unit 3* *unit 5*
8 Examining the **structure** of a poem	*unit 7* *unit 8*
9 Noticing **storytelling** techniques – such as building tension	*unit 4* *unit 7*
10 Exploring **sentence structure** – the way meaning is constrained within lines or flows across line-ends	*unit 4* *unit 7* *unit 8*
11 Noticing **development** within the writer's ideas or arguments	*unit 7* *unit 8*
12 **Reading beneath the surface** – noticing irony, contradictions, hints	*unit 6* *unit 8*
13 Becoming confident in discussing different poetry **genres** – for example, lyric and narrative poems	*unit 8* *unit 9*
14 **Comparing** poems systematically	*unit 9*
15 **Writing** about poetry in an appropriate style, supporting points with evidence	*unit 8* *unit 9*

Unit 3 Poems about creatures	SKILLS CHECKLIST	SPECIAL FEATURES
'Hyena' *by Edwin Morgan*	*personal response* *vocabulary* *poetry/prose*	
'Town Owl' *by Laurie Lee*	*understanding* *vocabulary* *rhythm*	**Language panel:** *Syllable*
'The Lion and Albert' *by Marriott Edgar*	*rhythm* *narrative voice* *rhyme*	**Language panel:** *Rhyme scheme*
'The Fallow Deer at the Lonely House' *by Thomas Hardy*	*understanding* *structure* *personal response*	*PRE-1900*
'The Kraken' *by Alfred, Lord Tennyson*	*understanding* *vocabulary* *interpretations*	*PRE-1900*
'Lone Dog' *by Irene McLeod*	*understanding*	**CLOSE READING**

Unit 4 Mysterious poems	SKILLS CHECKLIST	SPECIAL FEATURES
'The Haunted Lift' *by James Kirkup*	*understanding* *vocabulary* *structure*	**Language panel:** *Associations*
'Prince Kano' *by Edward Lowbury*	*understanding* *rhyme*	**Language panel:** *Rhyming couplets*
'Far Over the Misty Mountains' *by J. R. R. Tolkien*	*understanding* *syntax* *vocabulary*	**Language panel:** *Adjectives* *Nouns* *Synonyms*
'The Survivors' *by R. S. Thomas*	*narrative voice* *understanding* *poetry/prose*	
'The Way through the Woods' *by Rudyard Kipling*	*understanding* *rhyme* *vocabulary*	*PRE-1900* **Language panel:** *Internal rhyme*
'The Listeners' *by Walter de la Mare*	*understanding* *vocabulary*	**CLOSE READING**

Developing Poetry Skills

Unit 7 Narrative poems	SKILLS CHECKLIST	SPECIAL FEATURES
'A Case of Murder' *by Vernon Scannell*	*character* *images* *symbolism*	**Language panel:** *Symbolism*
'The Lake' *by Roger McGough*	*understanding* *narrative structure* *personal response*	
'Gelert, Llewelyn's Dog' *by W. R. Spencer*	*narrative structure* *age of language* *sound patterns*	*PRE-1900*
'Bishop Hatto' *by Robert Southey*	*structure* *verbs* *personal response*	*PRE-1900*
'Fable' *by Janos Pilinszky*	*understanding* *language study* *poetry/prose*	**CLOSE READING**

Unit 8 Lyric poems	SKILLS CHECKLIST	SPECIAL FEATURES
'Death of a Naturalist' *by Seamus Heaney*	*vocabulary/senses* *structure* *writing about poetry*	
'For a Five-Year-Old' *by Fleur Adcock*	*understanding* *structure* *narrative voice*	
'Full Moon and Little Frieda' *by Ted Hughes*	*images* *audience* *lyric form*	
'Elegy' *by Chidiock Tichborne*	*images* *structure* *narrative voice*	*PRE-1900* **Language panel:** *Paradox*
'The Smell of Chrysanthemums' *by Elizabeth Jennings*	*understanding* *genre study*	**CLOSE READING**

Unit	Comparisons	SKILLS CHECKLIST
9	**'Being-in-love'** *by Roger McGough*	*narrative voice* *vocabulary* *rhyme scheme* *personal response*
	'Stop all the clocks, cut off the telephone' *by W. H. Auden*	*images* *rhythm* *personal response*
		Comparisons *writing about* *the poems*
	'Rabbit in mixer survives' *Daily Telegraph*	*understanding* *language features*
	'Rabbit in mixer survives' *by Roger McGough*	*understanding* *structure* *verse form*
		Comparisons *writing about* *the texts*
	A Night to Remember *by Walter Lord*	*genre study*
	Every Man for Himself *by Beryl Bainbridge*	*genre study*
	'The Convergence of the Twain' *by Thomas Hardy*	*understanding* *genre study*
		Comparisons *writing about* *the texts*

Poems about people

Starting Points

Poems can do anything – tell stories, describe people and events,
entertain, anger or baffle us. The poems in this unit are united by theme.
They all describe people in different ways.

You Being Born *by Brian Jones*

Being born is something we all have in common, although none of us
remembers it. Nine months of learning and growing in a safe, watery den ...
then suddenly we were catapulted into the bright light of the world. What was
it like for us? And what is it like for a parent to witness the miracle of birth?

You Being Born

I saw you born.
It was remarkable.
You shot out from between your mother's legs
like a rugby ball from a scrum
5   and the stocky Geordie midwife caught you neatly
and cried 'Whoops! She's come!'

You had a wrinkled jammy head
and spasmy legs like a portly frog's.
From your belly button a white root waved
10 that had fed you all the months you'd grown

and ripened in your mother's womb.
And let me tell you – I'm ashamed –
I forgot your mother completely – she had been
those things to me that one day you'll discover
15 in someone else, and think 'God, this is it!'
– My sweetheart, my warm dear, my red hot lover –

But for those moments, as the doctor
shoved cotton wool up your flat nose
and swabbed your eyes and cleaned your bum
20 I forgot completely all my life and love
and watched you like a pool of growing light
and whispered to myself 'She's come! She's come!'

Word Bank

Geordie – someone who
comes from Tyneside

spasmy – a made-up
word suggesting jerky
movement

portly – overweight

ACTIVITIES

1 Narrator

What picture do you get of the narrator as you read the poem? What is he like? What are his feelings? What are the different emotions he is feeling at this moment – for example, his feelings about the child and her mother? Use a spider diagram to write down some key words to describe him. Look closely at some of the words and phrases below to help build up a complete picture.

> **Narrator**
> As in a novel, the narrator is the person who tells you a story. In this poem we are told of the birth by the narrator – the person who is 'I'.

- It was remarkable
- I'm ashamed
- I forgot completely ... and whispered to myself

2 Images

The poem shows us some interesting images of what the new baby looks like. For each of the extracts below, say what picture it creates in your mind. Focus in particular on the words that have been underlined.

> **Image**
> The way a writer uses language to create a more powerful picture in our minds. Most often this is done by comparing one thing with another – 'like a rugby ball from a scrum'.

a 'You shot out from between your mother's legs
   <u>like a rugby ball from a scrum</u>'

b 'You had a <u>wrinkled jammy head</u>
   and <u>spasmy legs like a portly frog's</u>'

c 'From your belly button a <u>white root waved</u>
   <u>that had fed you all the months you'd grown</u>'

3 Personal response

With a friend, discuss what you like and dislike about the poem. Which parts are most entertaining or stick most in your mind? Which words and images are most successful or least successful? What do you think the poem shows us about the feelings of having a baby?

Write a brief letter to the author of the poem saying what you like and dislike about it. Start like this:

> Date
>
> Dear Brian Jones
> I am writing to give you my response to your poem, You Being Born ...

4 Options

Look at this comment from a Year 7 student:

'I like the poem, but I find it odd. The narrator seems really excited about the birth of his new daughter, and yet he uses very surprising descriptions – such as "like a rugby ball". I'd have thought he would describe her in a more respectful way to show his admiration for the new child.'

Write a paragraph saying whether you agree or disagree with all or parts of this statement. Support your ideas by referring back to words and phrases in the poem.

In Mrs Tilscher's Class *by Carol Ann Duffy*

One of the most important influences upon us in our early years is our schoolteacher. We often remember our teachers for years – the things they say and do (positive and negative), their enthusiasms and interests, their values.

Think of a teacher who has made an impact on you. What was s/he like? Think of a key memory you still hold. Try to sum up what it is that has made this person such a strong influence on you.

Word Bank

Blue Nile – river in east Africa, around 1500 km long

Tana – lake in north-east Ethiopia, the source of the Blue Nile

Ethiopia – state in north-east Africa

Khartoum – capital of the Sudan, at the junction of the Blue and White Nile rivers

Aswân – a town in south-east Egypt; also the location of a huge dam and reservoir

enthralling – gripping, fascinating

Brady and Hindley – the 'Moors Murderers' Ian Brady and Myra Hindley were imprisoned for the murder of children on Saddleworth Moor, Cheshire, in 1966.

dunce – idiot

appalled – full of horror

tangible – able to be touched

fractious – bad tempered

In Mrs Tilscher's Class

You could travel up the Blue Nile
with your finger, tracing the route
while Mrs Tilscher chanted the scenery.
Tana. Ethiopia. Khartoum. Aswân.
5 That for an hour, then a skittle of milk
and the chalky Pyramids rubbed into dust.
A window opened with a long pole.
The laugh of a bell swung by a running child.

This was better than home. Enthralling books.
10 The classroom glowed like a sweet shop.
Sugar paper. Coloured shapes. Brady and Hindley
faded, like the faint, uneasy smudge of a mistake.
Mrs Tilscher loved you. Some mornings, you found
she'd left a good gold star by your name.
15 The scent of a pencil slowly, carefully, shaved.
A xylophone's nonsense heard from another form.

Over the Easter term, the inky tadpoles changed
from commas into exclamation marks. Three frogs
hopped in the playground, freed by a dunce,
20 followed by a line of kids, jumping and croaking
away from the lunch queue. A rough boy
told you how you were born. You kicked him, but stared
at your parents, appalled, when you got back home.

That feverish July, the air tasted of electricity.
25 A tangible alarm made you always untidy, hot,
fractious under the heavy, sexy sky. You asked her
how you were born and Mrs Tilscher smiled,
then turned away. Reports were handed out.
You ran through the gates, impatient to be grown,
30 as the sky split open into a thunderstorm.

ACTIVITIES

1 Classroom details

The poem contains some details of objects and activities which seem typical of life in a primary school. Some tell us about *when* the poem is set. Others show how lively and happy the school is. Look at the list of details below and see whether you agree (✓) or disagree (✗) that they are part of *your* memory of primary school, too.

a milk

b a window opened by a long pole

c a bell swung by a child

d sugar paper

e coloured shapes

f gold stars

g the scent of a pencil carefully shaved

h xylophones

i tadpoles

j lunch queue

2 Character

a The poem starts off full of admiration for Mrs Tilscher. What does the poet admire and respect about her? Make a list of points about Mrs Tilscher's character.

b By the end of the poem, the writer's attitude has changed. Why have her feelings about Mrs Tilscher altered so dramatically?

3 Tone

The tone of the early part of the poem stresses how happy life in Mrs Tilscher's class is. But look again at lines 11 and 12:

> ... Brady and Hindley/
> faded, like the faint,
> uneasy smudge of a mistake.

Using the Word Bank to help you, think about why the writer has included this detail. What does it tell us about the experience of being in Mrs Tilscher's classroom?

> **Tone**
> This describes the writer's voice – whether it is serious, humorous, neutral, sarcastic and so on. The tone of a poem might change as it develops.

4 Another viewpoint

When Mrs Tilscher is asked about how we are born, she turns away. Why do you think this is?

Imagine a student writes to Mrs Tilscher many years after this event takes place, asking about her response. Write a short reply from Mrs Tilscher explaining why she behaved as she did.

You might begin:

Date

Dear (your name)
Thank you very much for your letter. It was lovely to hear from you again. Yes, I do remember the afternoon in class you mentioned ...

My Parents Kept me from Children who were Rough *by Stephen Spender*

When we are very young, our parents like to protect us from people. 'Never talk to strangers,' they say. They worry about who we might mix with, who our friends are. As we get older we become more independent. We might even want friends who our parents wouldn't really approve of.

In the last poem, Carol Ann Duffy showed us how *she* changed and how her attitude to her teacher changed. In this poem, see what you learn about the feelings of the narrator.

Word Bank

lithe – graceful in movement

My Parents Kept me from Children who were Rough

My parents kept me from children who were rough
And who threw words like stones and who wore torn clothes.
Their thighs showed through rags. They ran in the street
And climbed cliffs and stripped by the country streams.

5   I feared more than tigers their muscles like iron
And their jerking hands and their knees tight on my arms.
I feared the salt coarse pointing of those boys
Who copied my lisp behind me on the road.

They were lithe, they sprang out behind hedges
10   Like dogs to bark at our world. They threw mud
And I looked another way, pretending to smile.
I longed to forgive them, yet they never smiled.

ACTIVITIES

1 People

What impression do you get of the narrator of the poem? What impression do you get of the rough children?

Using a table with two columns – one headed 'Narrator' and the other 'Rough children' – list the points about the different people in the poem. Here are some hints to help you.

Narrator

- What do we learn about his background?

- How does he behave in the presence of the rough children?

- Why does he long to forgive them?

The children

- How do they speak?

- What do they wear?

- What do they do that seems exciting to the narrator?

- How do they seem tough and dangerous?

- How can you tell that they tease the narrator?

2 Images

The poet uses images to build a stronger impression of the rough children. Look at the images below and, for each one, describe the impression it gives. The first is done for you as an example.

Image	Impression of the children
threw words like stones (line 2)	their language is harsh and used to hurt people
their muscles like iron (line 5)	
they sprang out behind hedges / Like dogs to bark at our world (lines 9–10)	

3 Discussion points

a If the narrator and the children are so different, discuss why is he fascinated by them. If what they do is wrong, why is he so keen to be a part of their lives?

b Who do you think the poet is writing his poem for – the rough children, himself, an unknown audience? What do you see as the purpose of the poem – to warn against bullying, simply to describe what happened to himself, to entertain us ...?

Small Incident in Library
by David Sutton

The younger we are, the more we depend on our parents. But as we get older we want more independence. During this stage things can sometimes go wrong.

Think of a time when you got lost or separated from your parents. Where was it? How did it happen? How did you feel? If you were re-telling this event through a poem, whose viewpoint would you use – yours, or your parents'? What difference would that make to the final poem?

Small Incident in Library

The little girl is lost among the books.
Two years old maybe, in bobble cap,
White lacy tights, red coat. She stands and looks.
'Can't see you, Mummy.' Mummy, next row up,
5 Intent on reading answers absently:
'I'm here, love.' Child calls out again: 'Can't see.'

A large man, his intentions of the best,
Stoops: 'Where's Mummy, then?' Child backs away.
Now the tall shelves threaten like a forest.
10 She toddles fast between them, starts to cry,
Takes the next aisle down and as her mother
Rounds one end disappears behind the other.

I catch the woman's tired-eyed prettiness.
We smile, shake heads. The child comes back in sight,
15 Hurtles to her laughing, hugs her knees:
'Found you!', in such ringing pure delight
It fills the room, there's no one left who's reading.
The mother looks down, blinking. 'Great soft thing.'

Word Bank

intent on – concentrating on
absently – vaguely
intentions – aims

ACTIVITIES

1 People

In the poem we get pictures of two main people – the little girl and her mother. What do we learn about them – what they look like, their backgrounds (such as age), and the way they behave? Using a table with two columns – one headed 'Girl' and the other 'Mother' – make notes on the two people.

2 Exploring details

Look more closely at the second section of the poem, where the child is most frightened about being lost. Use the questions below to explore how the writer shows the girl's fear.

a Why does the large man bend down?

b Why does the girl back away?

c How can we tell that the man is trying to help?

d Why do you think the writer gives us so little detail about what the man looks like – apart from the fact that he is large?

e Why do you think the writer compares the shelves to 'a forest' (line 9)?

3 Poetry/prose

What makes 'Small Incident in Library' a poem? Look at the version that follows, which is written in prose rather than poetry.

> **Prose**
> Prose is the writing we see most – in newspapers, magazines, novels and leaflets. Prose is organised in sentences and paragraphs, whereas poetry is in lines and (usually) verses or stanzas. The language of poetry is usually more patterned.

The little girl is lost among the books. She is perhaps two years old, wearing a bobble hat, white lacy tights and a red coat. She stands and looks. 'Can't see you, Mummy,' she says. Her mother is in the next row up. She wants to continue reading but looks up and says, absently, 'I'm here, love.' The child calls out again: 'Can't see.'

Compare this version with the first section of the poem. What differences do you notice? How does it look different on the page? How does it feel different as you read it? Describe the differences you notice as precisely as possible.

Now take the next section of the poem and write it as if it were a paragraph in a story. Which words would you change? How would you alter the punctuation? How does the text feel different?

The Minnow Catching Boys
by Susan Skinner

Poets often use people and events from the past as their subjects. The memory of one person can often trigger similar feelings in the reader. In this poem, Susan Skinner remembers watching a group of children catching minnows – tiny fish found in ponds and canals. Her poem doesn't tell us much about who the boys are. Instead it uses her memory of them to create a powerful scene from the past.

What are your key memories of childhood? How would you begin to describe one scene that sticks in your mind? Would it be with the weather, who you were with or what happened?

Word Bank

waylay – lie in wait for

sense of immortality – feeling of living for ever

cascade – waterfall

The Minnow Catching Boys

By the bridge the sunburnt boys,
knee-deep, with yellow nets on sticks,
waylay the silky edge of water,
scan and dip.

5   Heads down, brown necks glistening
they make bets, poke and tip
their nimble catch.
Then one boy delicately lifts

his net and treads
10   the wet ridges of stone
to the dry pebbles, flips
his minnows into a tin bucket

and wades back slowly, alone
with a sense of immortality.
15   For they have always been here,
the minnow catching boys,

breeches rolled, hands cupped,
feet green in the shallows,
followed by an old dog bearing
20   a stick from ear to ear

and a small girl
who can never quite catch up,
calling for them to wait.
But no-one waits.

25   The dog paddles to the beach,
shakes in a cascade of diamonds
then wanders off.
Shadows under the bridge unfurl

and slip down river; the slow
30   sun dips behind trees
in a green burying.
And when they have had enough

the minnow catching boys
make for home, swinging
35   the tin bucket, shouldering nets
that glint like yellow butterflies in tow.

ACTIVITIES

1 Setting

The writer describes a memorable scene. Re-read the poem carefully and draw a quick sketch of what the poem describes. Label each detail to show what is happening – for example, based on the first line you might sketch the bridge and the boys, with the labels 'bridge' and 'boys – sunburnt'.

2 People

The poem describes a group of boys catching minnows. By the end of it, what have we learnt about the boys? Use a spider diagram like the one below to make notes on what they look like and what they do.

3 Images

The poet uses some vivid images (word pictures). Look at those listed below and discuss or write about the picture each one creates in your mind.

a 'the silky edge of water' (line 3)

b 'the dog ... shakes in a cascade of diamonds' (lines 25–6)

c 'the slow / sun dips behind trees / in a green burying' (lines 29–31)

d 'shouldering nets / that glint like yellow butterflies in tow' (lines 35–6)

4 More meanings

Looking at the boys, the poet says that they have:

... a sense of immortality.
For they have always been here (lines 14–15)

Discuss what you think she means by this.

CLOSE READING

Dad *by Elaine Feinstein*

Elaine Feinstein writes
about the death of her father ...

Dad

Your old hat hurts me, and those black
    fat raisins you like to press into
my palm from your soft heavy hand:
    I see you staggering back up the path
5 with sacks of potatoes from some local farm,
    fresh eggs, flowers. Every day I grieve

for your great heart broken and you gone.
    You loved to watch the trees. This year
you did not see their Spring.
10   The sky was freezing over the fen
as on that somewhere secretly appointed day
    you beached: cold, white-faced, shivering.

What happened, old bull, my loyal
    hoarse-voiced warrior? The hammer
15 blow that stopped you in your track
    and brought you to a hospital monitor
could not destroy your courage
    to the end you were
uncowed and unconcerned with pleasing anyone.

20 I think of you now as once again safely
    at my mother's side, the earth as
chosen as a bed, and feel most sorrow for
    all that was gentle in
my childhood buried there
25   already forfeit, now forever lost.

Word Bank

fen – flat, marshy land

beached – washed onto
the beach

forfeit – confiscated

24

CLOSE READING

Advice on reading

This section develops your ability to respond to the language of a single poem. Start by reading the poem through once, perhaps jotting down notes about your first impressions. Then look at the questions below. What areas are you being asked to focus on? Now read the poem carefully once more, again making notes of ideas that occur to you. Remember that responding to an unseen poem will often require you to read it through carefully three or more times.

Advice on writing

Remember to answer each question in a full sentence or paragraph. Support your ideas with examples from the text wherever possible. Try to quote just a few words at a time rather than copying out chunks of the text.

Questions

a What do you think the writer means in line 1 when she says: 'Your old hat hurts me'?

b What impression do you get of the father from the lines: '... old bull, my loyal / hoarse-voiced warrior?' (lines 13–14)?

c What was the father like, even to the end of his life?

d Choose a phrase or line that you think shows the writer's emotions. Write it down, then write a sentence about why you chose it.

e Who do you think the writer is writing the poem for – an unknown audience, or for herself?

  ● How can you tell?

  ● How would you describe the purpose of her poem?

f Write a paragraph on the impressions you get of the narrator of the poem. What is she like? How is she feeling? What has her relationship with her father been like?

Poems about places

Starting Points

Carefully chosen words, sharp images and powerful use of the senses can make us feel as if we really are in a different world. The poems in this unit all explore places – some haunting and different, some lost for ever, some that we might recognise.

The Toadstool Wood *by James Reeves*

James Reeves describes a place that feels dark and mysterious. It is a wood where your imagination starts to think that there are more than trees and plants alive ...

Word Bank

stilted – long legs make it appear to be walking on stilts

uncanny – strange

The Toadstool Wood

The toadstool wood is dark and mouldy,
    And has a ferny smell.
About the trees hangs something quiet
    And queer—like a spell.

5 Beneath the arching sprays of bramble
    Small creatures make their holes;
Over the moss's close green velvet
    The stilted spider strolls.

The stalks of toadstools pale and slender
10   That grow from that old log,
Bars they might be to imprison
    A prince turned to a frog.

There lives no mumbling witch nor wizard
    In this uncanny place,
15 Yet you might think you saw at twilight
    A little, crafty face.

ACTIVITIES

1 Opinions

Look at these differing opinions from two Year 7 pupils.

Craig	Ellie
The wood is mysterious, but not really nasty.	It is! The language keeps showing us that it's really unpleasant.

Working in pairs, imagine what arguments Craig and Ellie could each use to support their points of view. Which parts of the poem could they use as evidence? Make a list of points for each side. Then decide which statement – Craig's or Ellie's – you most agree with.

2 Senses

One way that the writer brings the scene alive is by making readers use their senses – in particular imagining sights, sounds and smells.

Look through the poem to find examples of sight words, sound words and smell words, using a table like the one below. Against each word place a tick (✓) or a cross (✗) to show whether you think it has a pleasant or unpleasant effect. An example is done for you.

Sight	Sound	Smell
dark ✗	mumbling ✗	ferny ✓

You'll probably find some words where it's not easy to say whether they create a positive or negative effect. 'Mumbling' (shown in the Sound column) is an example. Once you have completed the table, compare your response with a friend's. See whether you agree or disagree about the sense words the writer has used.

3 Changing the effect

Using the list of sense words you have made, change each one for a different sense word in the same category to try to alter the overall effect. For example:

take dark (✗) and change it to another sight word, but this time one with a positive effect (✓). So you might choose light, bright or clear.

Do the same for your other words. Then, as a class, listen to the different effects of the poem when it is read aloud in all these different versions.

Stopping by Woods on a Snowy Evening

by Robert Frost

This description of woods is one of the most haunting and beautiful poems ever written. People respond to it in different ways. Some see it as a brilliant description of winter. Others feel that it describes perfectly the feelings you have in the middle of a long journey. Others find it more difficult to pinpoint its meaning. See what you think.

Word Bank

downy – like a feather

Stopping by Woods on a Snowy Evening

Whose woods these are I think I know.
His house is in the village, though;
He will not see me stopping here
To watch his woods fill up with snow.

5 My little horse must think it queer
To stop without a farmhouse near
Between the woods and frozen lake
The darkest evening of the year.

He gives his harness bells a shake
10 To ask if there is some mistake
The only other sound's the sweep
Of easy wind and downy flake.

The woods are lovely, dark, and deep,
But I have promises to keep,
15 And miles to go before I sleep,
And miles to go before I sleep.

ACTIVITIES

1 Narrator

What do we learn about the person who narrates (or speaks) the poem? Use the questions below to explore the character of the narrator.

a How can you tell that the narrator knows the place where s/he has stopped?

b How can you tell that this is not the end of the narrator's journey?

c Why do you think s/he stops here?

d What feelings does the narrator have as s/he looks into the woods?

e What do you think the 'promises' might be?

f Who do you think the narrator is and where might s/he be heading?

g Do you think the narrator is a 'he' or a 'she'?

2 Place

Look more closely at the impression we get of the place where the narrator has halted. It contains some of these features:

- woods
- house
- village
- road
- frozen lake.

Draw a map of what you think the scene is like – where the narrator has stopped, and where the other features of the scene are. Compare your impression with a friend's. Keep referring back to the poem for as many clues as possible.

3 Poetry and prose

Even if you weren't reading this text in a book of poetry, you would quickly know that it was a poem. It has a strong, steady rhythm, a pattern of rhyme, patterns of sounds ('The woods are lovely, dark, and deep' – line 13) and a repeated final rhyme.

How do these ingredients make the poem feel mysterious?

To start to feel how the special ingredients of the poem work, look at what it would be like if it were written in prose (everyday language). Below is a prose version of the opening lines. Continue it, trying to make it sound as much as possible like modern everyday English. Then write a paragraph describing what changes you have made and how the atmosphere in the two versions feels different.

> I think I know whose woods these are, but his house is in the village. He won't see me stopping here to watch his woods fill up with snow.

PRE-1900

The Trees Are Down by Charlotte Mew

Sometimes we remember places not for what they are like, but for
something that happened there. This poem by Charlotte Mew is like that.
She recalls a place that is being destroyed by human beings. In her poem
she reflects on what the place was once like ... and how it has become.

The Trees Are Down

– and he cried with a loud voice:
Hurt not the earth, neither the sea, nor the trees –

(Revelation)

They are cutting down the great plane trees at the end of the gardens.
For days there has been the grate of the saw, the swish of the branches as they fall,
The crash of trunks, the rustle of trodden leaves,
With the "Whoops" and the "Whoas", the loud common talk, the loud
5 common laughs of the men, above it all.

I remember one evening of a long past spring
Turning in at a gate, getting out of a cart, and finding a large dead rat in the
mud of the drive.
I remember thinking: alive or dead, a rat was a god-forsaken thing,
10 But at least, in May, that even a rat should be alive.

The week's work here is as good as done. There is just one bough
  On the roped bole, in the fine grey rain,
      Green and high
      And lonely against the sky.
        (Down now! –)
15   And but for that,
      If an old dead rat
Did once, for a moment, unmake the spring, I might never have thought of
him again.

20 It is not for a moment the spring is unmade today;
These were great trees, it was in them from root to stem:
When the men with the "Whoops" and the "Whoas" have carted the whole of
the whispering loveliness away
Half the spring, for me, will have gone with them.

25 It is going now, and my heart has been struck with the hearts of the planes:
Half my life it has beat with these, in the sun, in the rains,
    In the March wind, the May breeze,
  In the great gales that came over to them across the roofs from the great seas.
      There was only a quiet rain when they were dying;
      They must have heard the sparrows flying,
30 And the small creeping creatures in the earth where they were lying –
      But I, all day, I heard an angel crying:
        "Hurt not the trees."

Word Bank

plane trees –
tall trees with
decorative,
peeling bark

god-forsaken
– outcast

bole –
tree-trunk

ACTIVITIES

1 Sounds

In the first section of the poem, Charlotte Mew uses onomatopoeic words to help the reader imagine the destruction of the trees. Look at the examples listed below and, for each one, try to describe the effect it creates as you read it. The first one is done for you as an example.

> **Onomatopoeic**
> These are words that sound like the sounds they describe – crash, buzz, murmur, crack. We use them because they can make descriptions seem more vivid.

Onomatopoeic word	Effect
<u>grate</u> of the saw (line 2)	*a harsh sound, to show that something vicious is taking place*
<u>swish</u> of the branches	
the <u>crash</u> of trunks	
<u>rustle</u> of trodden leaves	
'<u>Whoops</u>' and the '<u>Whoas</u>'	

2 Attitudes

Look at the attitude of the men in the poem as they cut down the trees. What can you tell about their feelings for the trees? Compare this with the narrator's views – especially in the final section. What do you learn about her feelings now that the trees have gone? Why do you think she is so affected by the event?

3 Language

'The Trees Are Down' is one of the older poems in this book. Could you tell this as you read it? Working as a time detective, look for some clues about its age.

There are hints in the content (i.e. things that happen in the poem) and in the language. Look at the examples opposite and, for each one, say how it suggests the age of the poem.

Content clues

a 'Turning in at a gate, getting out of a cart ...' (line 8)

Language clues

a '... my heart has been struck with the hearts of the planes' (line 26)

b 'I remember one evening of a long past spring' (line 7)

c 'Hurt not the trees' (line 34)

Are there any other clues you can find to the age of the poem?

Pompeii *by Judith Nicholls*

24th August, AD 79 seemed like any other day in a long, hot Italian summer. But as one eyewitness later said: 'In the early afternoon, my mother drew my attention to a cloud of unusual size and appearance.' Within hours Mount Vesuvius, a terrifyingly powerful volcano, had erupted, sending out 'broad sheets of fire and leaping flames'. The ash and lava from the eruption buried the towns of Pompeii and Herculaneum, killing thousands of people. Judith Nicholls uses poetry to capture the scene.

Pompeii

The giants are sleeping now
under a hot land
where the grey snow
has yet to fall
5   and cover all
with its dying dew.

The city is silent now
under a haze of blue
till the pedlar's cart
10   on the stone-clad street
calls the early few
for pot or shoe
and the slave from sleep.

The hillside is sunwashed now
15   where the lush vine
and the olives line
the summer's slopes
of the giants' home
in an August dream
20   that has almost gone.

The gods are sleeping now
unaware
by the temple walls
and market stalls
25   of the city square...

And an ashen cloud
shrouds the breathless crowd
as the grey snow falls.

ACTIVITIES

1 Understanding

The first four verses of the text describe the city of Pompeii before the deadly ash begins to fall. What picture of the city does Judith Nicholls create? What details does she give about what life there must have been like?

2 Language clues

The events in the poem are almost 2,000 years old. How can you tell that the poem is set in the past? What details help to make it feel like a different world?

3 Structure

Look at the first line of the first four verses. It always ends with 'now'. Why do you think this might be? What if the poem were re-written in the past tense, using the adverb 'then' instead of 'now'? The first verse would sound like this:

The giants <u>were</u> sleeping <u>then</u>
under a hot land
where the grey snow
<u>had</u> yet to fall
and cover all
with its dying dew.

The changes to the tense of the language are underlined. Now do the same to the rest of the poem. Think about how this makes the poem different. Why do you think Judith Nicholls has chosen to use the present tense?

4 Images

The writer uses some memorable visual images to help us imagine the scene. Look at the list of images below and, for each one, describe the picture it creates in your mind.

Adverbs

Adverbs tell us more about the verb. They show when, how or where something happens, like this:

verb	adverb
run	quickly
eat	noisily

These are easy adverbs to spot because they end in -ly. But there are other, less recognisable, adverbs which tell us about time, manner and place – such as <u>often</u>, <u>now</u>, <u>yesterday</u>, <u>then</u>; <u>quite</u>, <u>even</u>, <u>nevertheless</u>; <u>there</u>, <u>here</u>.

---

a 'The giants are sleeping now' (line 1)

b 'dying dew' (line 6)

c 'The hillside is sunwashed' (line 14)

d 'an ashen cloud / shrouds the breathless crowd' (lines 26–7)

e 'the grey snow' (line 28)

PRE-1900

Lines Composed in a Wood on a Windy Day

by Anne Brontë

The Brontë family – Emily, Charlotte, Anne, Branwell and their father, Patrick – lived early last century in a bleak, isolated spot called Haworth on the Yorkshire Moors. On one side the windows of their parsonage gave them a view of moorland and hills that stretched for miles; on the other side, they looked into a dark graveyard.

Their environment would haunt their writing. In this poem, Anne Brontë describes a windy day as if their stone house is out at sea.

Lines Composed in a Wood on a Windy Day

My soul is awakened, my spirit is soaring
And carried aloft on the wings of the breeze;
For above and around me the wild wind is roaring,
Arousing to rapture the earth and the seas.

5 The long withered grass in the sunshine is glancing,
The bare trees are tossing their branches on high;
The dead leaves, beneath them, are merrily dancing,
The white clouds are scudding across the blue sky.

I wish I could see how the ocean is lashing
10 The foam of its billows to whirlwinds of spray;
I wish I could see how its proud waves are dashing,
And hear the wild roar of their thunder to-day!

Word Bank
aloft – upwards
arousing – waking
rapture – excitement
scudding – drifting quickly

ACTIVITIES

1 Vocabulary

Some people describing a storm in a wood might be terrified. They might show its frightening power. Anne Brontë gives a positive picture of the storm. Using two columns, as in the table below, pick out the words she uses that show the power of the storm and her positive feelings about it. An example of each is done for you.

Power of the storm	Her positive feelings
wild wind	my soul is awakened

2 Narrator

What picture of the narrator do you get from the poem? Which of these words best describes her and why?

- happy
- optimistic
- excited
- scared
- religious
- observant

3 Sounds

Anne Brontë's poem helps us to imagine the power of the storm through the rhythm and sounds she uses. Working in small groups, put together a performance that emphasises its sound. You could perform one verse or all of the poem using the following 'techniques':

- whisper, mutter, shout some words
- say some words solo or as a whole group
- alternate who says each word – so that each member of the group says the next word in the line
- speak quickly or slowly
- change pace suddenly or gradually
- emphasise the alliteration in some lines
- make sound effects in the background.

> **Alliteration**
> Alliteration is a series of words that begin with the same sound. They help writers to create patterns in their language. Sometimes the words may be next to each other: '<u>a</u>bove <u>a</u>nd <u>a</u>round'; sometimes further apart: 'The white clouds are <u>sc</u>udding across the blue <u>sk</u>y'.

4 Rhythm kit

Anne Brontë's poem has a powerful rhythm which helps us to feel the atmosphere of the windy day. Working on your own or in a pair, try to write another verse of the poem using the same rhythm. To do this, you'll need to keep saying it aloud to yourself until it feels right. To get you started, you might use this opening line, then add three more of your own.

The gravestones are battered, the trees now are creaking ...

> **Rhythm**
> Rhythm is the pattern of sounds writers create through the words they use. Anne Brontë creates a fast-moving, thumping rhythm to emphasise the power of the wind. Judith Nicholls, in the last poem, used a much less obvious rhythm, giving her poem the feel of something more calm and tranquil. Rhythm in language works as in music: different beats are put together in a certain pattern. You'll learn more about this in the 'Focus on Sounds' unit.

CLOSE READING

To the Sea

To the Sea *by Philip Larkin*

In this poem, Philip Larkin thinks back to the seaside memories of his childhood ...

To step over the low wall that divides
Road from concrete walk above the shore
Brings sharply back something known long before—
The miniature gaiety of seasides.
5 Everything crowds under the low horizon :
Steep beach, blue water, towels, red bathing caps,
The small hushed waves' repeated fresh collapse
Up the warm yellow sand, and further off
A white steamer stuck in the afternoon—

10 Still going on, all of it, still going on!
To lie, eat, sleep in hearing of the surf
(Ears to transistors, that sound tame enough
Under the sky), or gently up and down
Lead the uncertain children, frilled in white
15 And grasping at enormous air, or wheel
The rigid old along for them to feel
A final summer, plainly still occurs
As half an annual pleasure, half a rite,

As when, happy at being on my own,
20 I searched the sand for Famous Cricketers,
Or, farther back, my parents, listeners
To the same seaside quack, first became known.
Strange to it now, I watch the cloudless scene:
The same clear water over smoothed pebbles,
25 The distant bathers' weak protesting trebles
Down at its edge, and then the cheap cigars,
The chocolate-papers, tea-leaves, and, between

The rocks, the rusting soup-tins, till the first
Few families start the trek back to the cars.
30 The white steamer has gone. Like breathed-on glass
The sunlight has turned milky. If the worst
Of flawless weather is our falling short,
It may be that through habit these do best,
Coming to water clumsily undressed
35 Yearly ; teaching their children by a sort
Of clowning ; helping the old, too, as they ought.

Word Bank

gaiety – happiness
rite – ritual
quack – background noise
flawless – perfect

CLOSE READING

Advice on reading

This section develops your ability to respond to the language of a single poem. Start by reading the poem through once, perhaps jotting down notes about your first impressions. Then look at the questions below. What areas are you being asked to focus on? Now read the poem again more carefully, again making notes of ideas that occur to you. Remember that responding to an unseen poem will often require you to read it through carefully three or more times.

Advice on writing

Remember to answer each question in a full sentence or paragraph. Support your ideas with examples from the text wherever possible. Try to quote just a few words at a time rather than copying out chunks of the text.

Questions

a Look again at the first verse. What details do you think are typical of the English seaside?

b In verse two why do you think the children are 'uncertain'?

c What picture do you see when the writer says the children are 'grasping at enormous air'?

d In verse three what do you think the writer means when he says 'my parents ... first became known'?

e '... Like breathed-on glass
The sunlight has turned milky.' (lines 30–31)
What do you see in this image?

f Does Philip Larkin look back at the scene with positive memories, or is he embarrassed? Write a brief paragraph giving your opinion. Support your points with evidence from the poem.

g Does this text feel like a poem, or does it read as a list of remembered images? What features can you find that make it feel either like a poem or a piece of prose writing?

Poems about creatures

Starting Points

Human beings and animals have always had a mixed relationship. On the one hand, we keep animals to educate or entertain us. On the other hand, we hunt them, kill them for food or fur, or just for fun. The poems in this unit allow us to see things from the animals' point of view.

Hyena *by Edwin Morgan*

Hyenas have a bad reputation. Think of the way they are presented in films like *The Lion King*, or in advertising campaigns about car crime. Edwin Morgan's poem gives a voice to the hyena.

Hyena

I am waiting for you.
I have been travelling all morning through the bush
and not eaten.
I am lying at the edge of the bush
5 on a dusty path that leads from the burnt-out kraal.
I am panting, it is midday, I found no water-hole.
I am very fierce without food and although my eyes
are screwed to slits against the sun
you must believe I am prepared to spring.

10 What do you think of me?
I have a rough coat like Africa.
I am crafty with dark spots
like the bush-tufted plains of Africa.
I sprawl as a shaggy bundle of gathered energy
15 like Africa sprawling in its waters.
I trot, I lope, I slaver, I am a ranger.
I hunch my shoulders. I eat the dead.

Do you like my song?
When the moon pours hard and cold on the veldt
20 I sing, and I am the slave of darkness.
Over the stone walls and the mud walls and the ruined places
and the owls, the moonlight falls.
I sniff a broken drum. I bristle. My pelt is silver.
25 I howl my song to the moon – up it goes.
Would you meet me there in the waste places?

Word Bank

kraal – a village of huts surrounded by a fence or wall

veldt – plains of Africa

pelt - animal skin

carrion – dead flesh

sinews – muscles

It is said I am a good match
for a dead lion. I put my muzzle
at his golden flanks, and tear. He
30 is my golden supper, but my tastes are easy.
I have a crowd of fangs, and I use them.
Oh and my tongue – do you like me
when it comes lolling out of my jaw
very long, and I am laughing?
35 I am not laughing.
But I am not snarling either, only
panting in the sun, showing you
what I grip
carrion with.

40 I am waiting
for the foot to slide,
for the heart to seize,
for the leaping sinews to go slack,
for the fight to the death to be fought to the death,
45 for a glazing eye and the rumour of blood.
I am crouching in my dry shadows
till you are ready for me.
My place is to pick you clean
and leave your bones to the wind.

ACTIVITIES

1 Opinions

Do you think the poem encourages us to
like or dislike the hyena? Using a table like
this one below, make a list of the positive
and negative points we gain from the
poem about hyenas.

Positive	Negative

Compare your list with a friend's. On
balance, how do you feel about the hyena?
What is the poet's attitude?

2 Point of view

Look at how the poet helps us to imagine
the hyena's character by using the pronoun
'I' rather than 'she' or 'he'. Try replacing 'I'
with 'she' or 'he'. Discuss how this makes
the poem feel different.

3 Poetry/prose

This text *looks* like a poem on the page
because of the way its lines are laid out.
But what if it was presented visually as
prose? Look at the first section of the
poem below, set as if it was an extract
from a story. What clues are there – if any
– that it's actually a poem?

I am waiting for you. I have been
travelling all morning through the bush
and not eaten. I am lying at the
edge of the bush on a dusty path
that leads from the burnt-out kraal.
I am panting, it is midday, I found no
water-hole. I am very fierce without
food and although my eyes are
screwed to slits against the sun you
must believe I am prepared to spring.

Town Owl
by Laurie Lee

The owl is one of nature's more mysterious creatures because we rarely see it. Laurie Lee's poem helps us to imagine not only its habits and behaviour, but also the sheer terror it creates as night falls and the time for hunting begins.

Word Bank

deadly nightshade – a poisonous plant with black berries

augur – someone who foretells the future from signs or omens

talons – claws

doom – certain death

Town Owl

On eves of cold, when slow coal fires,
rooted in basements, burn and branch,
brushing with smoke the city air;

When quartered moons pale in the sky,
5   and neons glow along the dark
like deadly nightshade on a briar;

Above the muffled traffic then
I hear the owl, and at his note
I shudder in my private chair.

10   For like an augur he has come
to roost among our crumbling walls,
his blooded talons sheathed in fur.

Some secret lure of time it seems
has called him from his country wastes
15   to hunt a newer wasteland here.

And where the candelabra swung
bright with the dancers' thousand eyes,
now his black, hooded pupils stare,

And where the silk-shoed lovers ran
20   with dust of diamonds in their hair,
he opens now his silent wing,

And, like a stroke of doom, drops down,
and swoops across the empty hall,
and pluck a quick mouse off the stair …

ACTIVITIES

1 Understanding

Use the questions below to explore your own understanding of the poem.

a How can you tell that it is autumn or winter?

b How can you tell that the poem takes place in a town or city?

c When the writer hears the owl, what effect does it have upon him?

d Why might the owl have moved from the countryside to the town?

e Where exactly does the owl hunt its prey?

2 Vocabulary

Owls are often presented as attractive creatures. Do you think Laurie Lee's poem creates a positive picture of the town owl or does it seem menacing? Look more closely at the poem and see what you think about words and phrases like these:

- '… and at his note / I shudder in my private chair' (lines 8–9)

- 'like an augur' (line 10)

- 'his blooded talons' (line 12)

- 'like a stroke of doom' (line 22)

What impression of the owl do you get from each of these lines?

3 Rhythm

The writer uses mostly simple vocabulary in his poem. He also uses lots of one-syllable words. Look, for example, at the final verse: every word except across and empty has one syllable. The most polysyllabic words seem to be used when he describes the world of humans – candelabra, dancers', thousand, diamonds.

Using the notes below and your own ideas, think about the effect of this pattern of words. How does it help to create an impression of the owl, and the difference between its world and ours?

> strong rhythm
> like a heartbeat?
> ominous, worrying feeling
> makes the owl seem single-minded,
> straightforward, determined
> like the ticking of a large clock?
> uncomplicated
> repetitive
> heavy

Write a two- or three-sentence paragraph to explain what you notice about the rhythm in the poem.

Syllable

We can break words down into single units of sound. For example, paper has two syllables – pap+er; difficult has three syllables – diff+i+cult. Words of one syllable are described as monosyllabic; words with many syllables are polysyllabic.

The Lion and Albert *by Marriott Edgar*

This poem is a bit of a cheat: it's about people as much as creatures, but it's included here because it's much loved. It became famous as a monologue – a speech delivered by a one person, in this case a comedian. Listen to it, read it aloud and then have a go yourself at telling the tragic tale of Albert and the Lion.

Word Bank

swell – fashionable person
somnolent – sleepy
vexed – cross
summonsed – charged by the police

The Lion and Albert

There's a famous seaside place called Blackpool,
    That's noted for fresh air and fun,
And Mr and Mrs Ramsbottom
    Went there with young Albert, their son.

5 A grand little lad was young Albert,
    All dressed in his best; quite a swell
With a stick with an 'orse's 'ead 'andle,
    The finest that Woolworth's could sell.

They didn't think much to the Ocean:
10   The waves, they was fiddlin' and small,
There was no wrecks and nobody drownded,
    Fact, nothing to laugh at at all.

So, seeking for further amusement,
    They paid and went into the Zoo,
15 Where they'd Lions and Tigers and Camels,
    And old ale and sandwiches too.

There were one great big Lion called Wallace;
    His nose were all covered with scars –
He lay in a somnolent posture
20   With the side of his face on the bars.

Now Albert had heard about Lions,
    How they were ferocious and wild –
To see Wallace lying so peaceful,
    Well, it didn't seem right to the child.

25 So straightway the brave little feller,
    Not showing a morsel of fear,
Took his stick with its 'orse's 'ead 'andle
    And poked it in Wallace's ear.

You could see that the Lion didn't like it,
30   For giving a kind of a roll,
He pulled Albert inside the cage with 'im,
    And swallowed the little lad 'ole.

Then Pa, who had seen the occurrence,
    And didn't know what to do next,
35 Said "Mother! Yon Lion's 'et Albert,"
    And Mother said "Well, I am vexed!"

So Mr and Mrs Ramsbottom –
    Quite rightly, when all's said and done –
Complained to the Animal Keeper
40   That the Lion had eaten their son.

The keeper was quite nice about it;
    He said "What a nasty mishap.
Are you sure that it's *your* boy he's eaten?"
    Pa said "Am I sure? There's his cap!"

45 The manager had to be sent for.
    He came and he said "What's to do?"
Pa said "Yon Lion's 'et Albert,
    And 'im in his Sunday clothes, too."

Then Mother said, "Right's right, young feller;
50   I think it's a shame and a sin
For a lion to go and eat Albert,
    And after we've paid to come in."

The manager wanted no trouble,
    He took out his purse right away,
55 Saying "How much to settle the matter?"
    And Pa said "What do you usually pay?"

But Mother had turned a bit awkward
    When she thought where her Albert had gone.
She said "No! someone's got to be summonsed" –
60   So that was decided upon.

Then off they went to the P'lice Station,
    In front of the Magistrate chap;
They told 'im what happened to Albert,
    And proved it by showing his cap.

65 The Magistrate gave his opinion
    That no one was really to blame
And he said that he hoped the Ramsbottoms
    Would have further sons to their name.

At that Mother got proper blazing,
70   "And thank you, sir, kindly," said she.
"What, waste all our lives raising children
    To feed ruddy Lions? Not me!"

ACTIVITIES

1 Characters

There are many different characters in the poem. We don't really get to know any of them well, but we do learn a little about the main people. Using the headings in the chart below, make a list of what we know about these characters.

Mr Ramsbottom	Mrs Ramsbottom	Albert	Wallace (the lion)
easy-going — doesn't want to make trouble		wearing his best clothes	nose covered in scars (a fighter?)

2 Rhythm

Practise reading the poem aloud. The best way is probably for everyone to take a part, like this:

- Narrator
- Mr Ramsbottom
- Mrs Ramsbottom
- the keeper
- the manager
- the magistrate.

The comedian who made it famous, Stanley Holloway, spoke the poem in a strong northern accent. You might try the same. You also need to think about ways of using the rhythm of the poem. Are you going to read it as if it's natural spoken language, or is that impossible? Should you place heavy emphasis on the poem's rhythm?

Discuss how you will present the text to best effect, then practise reading so that your performance flows well and everyone speaks at the right time. The main things to remember are the pace and style – so that the audience is entertained and amused.

3 Point of view

We don't learn much about Wallace, the boy-eating lion. Imagine his point of view. He's lying peacefully in his cage when an irritating child pokes a stick into his ear. As a result, he eats the boy. Try to write two or three verses of the poem (or more) from Wallace's point of view. Aim to get the same pattern of sounds as the original – the same strong, slow rhythm and a similar rhyme scheme – where the last word of the second and fourth lines rhyme.

You might start like this:

I was lying there minding my business,
When some people came up to my cage ...

Rhyme scheme

A rhyme scheme is the term used to describe the way a writer organises rhyming lines. In this poem there are four lines to a verse. The second and fourth lines rhyme (fun ... son).

If you write out the rhyme scheme, you usually use letters to show which lines rhyme with which. Each letter stands for a different rhyme. So the rhyme scheme for this poem would be:

A Blackpool
B fun
C Ramsbottom
B son

43

PRE-1900

The Fallow Deer at the Lonely House *by Thomas Hardy*

Thomas Hardy is known as a novelist and poet whose work spanned the nineteenth and twentieth centuries. During his long life (1840–1928) he wrote a number of novels and stories usually dealing with human relationships and conflict. Much of his work is deeply rooted in nature and the countryside of south-west England.

The poem on this page has been printed with the second verse scrambled. The rhyme scheme is printed beside the first verse. (For an explanation of how rhyme schemes work, see page 43.)

The poem has two verses, each with six lines. Both verses have the same rhyme scheme.

Using the first verse, the rhyme scheme and your own detective work to help you, see if you can place the lines of the second verse into an order that:

a makes sense
b matches the structure of verse 1.

The Fallow Deer at the Lonely House

One without looks in tonight	A
Through the curtain-chink	B
From the sheet of glistening white;	A
One without looks in tonight	A
As we sit and think	B
By the fender-brink.	B

Watching in the snow;
Wondering, aglow,
We do not discern those eyes
We do not discern those eyes
Fourfooted, tiptoe.
Lit by lamps of rosy dyes

Word Bank

fallow deer – small deer with red-brown coat
fender-brink – fireside
discern – notice
without – outside
aglow – glowing

You can check your answer against the original poem on page 128.

ACTIVITIES

1 Structure

Look at the complete text in the order Thomas Hardy wrote it (page 128). How close did you get to re-arranging the lines on page 44 correctly? Think about how you approached the task. What was your main method?

- Did you use the structure of verse 1 to guide you?
- Did you look at the rhyme scheme?
- Did you place the lines in an order that seemed to make most sense?
- Did you use complete guesswork?

Compare your approach with others in your class.

2 Understanding

Read the poem through again, this time concentrating on its meaning.

a Why do you think the deer has been drawn to the window of the house on this evening?

b What are the people inside doing?

c What thoughts do you imagine would be going through the deer's mind?

3 Viewpoints

Read these different views of the poem. Which do you most agree with and why?

a The poem shows humans admiring nature.

b It shows the way the worlds of humans and animals always stay separate.

c It shows the animal fascinated by, but afraid of, humans.

d It shows the animal observing the humans while the humans are totally unaware that the deer is there.

e It shows that animals wish to be like humans.

PRE-1900
The Kraken *by Alfred, Lord Tennyson*

This poem is about an imaginary creature that lives deep in the ocean ... until one day it awakens. It was written in the middle of the Victorian period, at a time when people were becoming increasingly interested in monsters and the beginnings of what we would now call science fiction. Mary Shelley's novel *Frankenstein* was written in 1818, and in 1869 the French novelist Jules Verne wrote a book called *20,000 Leagues under the Sea* (1 league = 3 miles), which imagined a submarine voyage to the uncharted depths of the ocean, and the kind of monstrous creatures that might live there.

Tennyson's poem describes such a creature, using poetry to create a sense of mystery and fascination.

The Kraken

Below the thunders of the upper deep;
Far, far beneath in the abysmal sea,
His ancient, dreamless, uninvaded sleep
The Kraken sleepeth; faintest sunlights flee
5 About his shadowy sides; above him swell
Huge sponges of millennial growth and height;
And far away into the sickly light,
From many a wondrous grot and secret cell
Unnumber'd and enormous polypi
10 Winnow with giant arms the slumbering green.
There hath he lain for ages and will lie
Battening upon huge seaworms in his sleep,
Until the latter fire shall heat the deep;
Then once by men and angels to be seen,
15 In roaring he shall rise and on the surface die.

Word Bank

abysmal – profoundly dreadful
millennial – a thousand years' worth
grot – cave
polypi – giant squid
winnow – stir
battening upon – clutching
latter – final

ACTIVITIES

1 Understanding

Use the questions below to aid your understanding of the poem.

a What clues are there in the poem about the age of the Kraken?

b What do we learn about the appearance of the Kraken?

c What will happen to the Kraken when he finally wakes up?

2 Language study

The poem is around 150 years old. Could you tell as you first read it? The words and phrases below, in particular, hint at its age. For each one, try to explain why it helps us to know that the poem is not modern.

Word(s)	Comment
sleepeth (line 4)	
Unnumber'd (line 9)	
There hath he lain (line 11)	
Until the latter fire shall ... (line 13)	

How do you react to the archaic (old-fashioned) words? Do they add to the atmosphere of the poem, or did they get in the way of your understanding?

3 Interpretations

Look again at the ending of the poem, and in particular these words:

'the latter fire shall heat' (line 13)

'angels' (line 14)

'rise' and 'die' (line 15)

The *Book of Revelation* – the final book of the Bible – describes the end of the world. It will be engulfed in fire ... Do you think this might be what Tennyson means by 'the latter fire'? What do you think he is saying here?

CLOSE READING

Lone Dog *by Irene McLeod*

Lone Dog

I'm a lean dog, a keen dog, a wild dog and lone,
I'm a rough dog, a tough dog, hunting on my own!
I'm a bad dog, a mad dog, teasing silly sheep;
I love to sit and bay the moon and keep fat souls from sleep.

5 I'll never be a lap dog, licking dirty feet,
A sleek dog, a meek dog, cringing for my meat.
Not for me the fireside, the well-filled plate,
But shut door and sharp stone and cuff and kick and hate.

Not for me the other dogs, running by my side,
10 Some have run a short while, but none of them would bide.
O mine is still the lone trail, the hard trail, the best,
Wide wind and wild stars and the hunger of the quest.

Word Bank

meek – quiet, well-behaved
cringing – bowing down low
bide – stay
quest – journey to find something

CLOSE READING

Advice on reading

This section develops your ability to respond to the language of a single poem. Start by reading the poem through once, perhaps jotting down notes about your first impressions. Then look at the questions below. What areas are you being asked to focus on? Now read the poem carefully once more, again making notes of ideas that occur to you. Remember that responding to an unseen poem will often require you to read it through carefully three or more times.

Advice on writing

Remember to answer each question in a full sentence or paragraph. Support your ideas with examples from the text wherever possible. Try to quote just a few words at a time rather than copying out chunks of the text.

Questions

Understanding

a   How can you tell that the lone dog is proud of himself?

b   What makes him different from other dogs?

c   What does the lone dog enjoy about his lifestyle?

d   How does Irene McLeod show that the lone dog belongs in nature?

e   What do you think the last part – 'the hunger of the quest' – means?

Style

f   Look at the repetition in the poem: 'lean dog', 'keen dog', 'wild dog', 'rough dog' ... and so on. Why do you think the writer repeats these phrases in this way?

g   The writer also uses repetition of initial sounds (alliteration): '... shut door and sharp stone and cuff and kick and hate' (line 8). How does this add to our impression of the lone dog?

h   Write a sentence or two describing the effect the rhythm of the poem has upon you.

Response

i   What do you like or dislike about the poem?

Mysterious poems

Starting Points

Poetry is good at creating mysteries because of the way it hints at things, as the poems in this unit show. The language of poetry can create impressions and feelings without always telling us the facts.

The Haunted Lift by *James Kirkup*

We often expect mysteries to be set in the past in certain places – churchyards or abandoned houses, perhaps. James Kirkup's poem is especially chilling because it is so modern and is set in such an unexpected location.

The Haunted Lift

On the ground floor
of this ultramodern
tower block

in the dead
5   middle
of the night

the lift doors
open, with a
clang.

10   Nobody enters,
and nobody
comes out.

In the dead
middle
15   of the night

the lift doors
close with a clang,
and the lift begins

to move
20   slowly
up . . .

with nobody in it,
nobody but
the ghost of a girl

25   who lived here once
on the thirteenth floor of
this ultramodern tower block.

One day, she went to play
in an old part of town,
30   and never came back.

She said she was just
going to the corner shop,
but she never came home.

Now her ghost
35   keeps pressing
in the dead

middle of the night
the button
for the thirteenth floor.

40   But when the door
opens with a clang
she cannot step out.

She gazes longingly
at the familiar landing,
45   but only for a moment . . .

then the lift doors
clang in her face
and her tears

silently flow
50   as the lift
in the dead

middle
of the night
so soft and slow

55   carries her down again
down below,
far, far below

the ground
floor, where nobody
60   waits for the haunted lift

in the dead
middle
of the night.

Sometimes
65   on the thirteenth floor
her mother and father

with her photo
beside their bed
wake up

70   in the dead
middle of the night, and hear
the mysterious clanging

of closing lift doors,
and wonder
75   who it could be

in the dead
middle
of the night

using the lift
80   at such
an unearthly hour.

In this ultramodern
tower block
there is no thirteenth floor.

ACTIVITIES

1 Fact finding

You are a detective and have been assigned to the case of the Haunted Lift. What are the facts – about the girl, the parents and the place? Make notes on what you can tell from the poem, using a chart like the one below.

Girl	Parents	Place

2 Vocabulary

James Kirkup creates a number of mysteries in the poem – like who the lost girl might be and why there can be no thirteenth floor. You'll probably enjoy coming up with your own theories about these.

Associations

Associations are the feelings certain words can create in us. The word 'black' is associated with death and evil. 'Light' is associated with clarity and truth. Associative words trigger our deeper thoughts and feelings. They are therefore very useful to poets because they can create a powerful emotional response in us.

Look also at the way he uses words that create a feeling of menace or uncertainty. Take the two words below and look at the way the writer uses them in the poem. For each one, use a spider diagram to brainstorm some of the associations each word has.

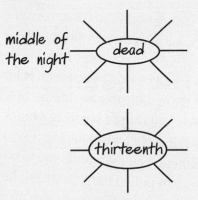

3 Structure

When we first read the poem, it seems like a list of ideas with a lot of repetition of certain words and phrases.

a If you were dividing the poem up into sections, how many would you have and what would each one be about?

b Do you feel that the repetition of words and phrases works well in the poem? Does it add to the suspense, or does it irritate you?

4 Editing

If you were to shorten the poem, by cutting out some of the repetitions, how would its effect change? Try it. If you have a word processor, type the text in and then use cut and paste to produce versions of different lengths.

a At what point does cutting the poem make it lose its impact?

b How does the overall effect of the poem change when you shorten it?

Prince Kano *by Edward Lowbury*

This text has a much more typical 'mystery' setting than the previous poem. It tells of someone lost in a dark wood and about to get a nasty surprise ...

Prince Kano

In a dark wood Prince Kano lost his way
And searched in vain through the long summer's day.
At last, when night was near, he came in sight
Of a small clearing filled with yellow light,
5   And there, bending beside his brazier, stood
A charcoal burner wearing a black hood.
The Prince cried out for joy: 'Good friend, I'll give
What you will ask: guide me to where I live.'
The man pulled back his hood: he had no face –
10 Where it should be there was an empty space.

Half dead with fear the Prince staggered away,
Rushed blindly through the wood till break of day;
And then he saw a large clearing, filled
With houses, people, but his soul was chilled;
15 He looked around for comfort, and his search
Led him inside a small, half-empty church
Where monks prayed. 'Father,' to one he said,
'I've seen a dreadful thing; I am afraid.'
'What did you see, my son?' 'I saw a man
20 Whose face was like ...' and, as the Prince began,
The monk drew back his hood and seemed to hiss,
Pointing to where his face should be, 'like this?'

Word Bank

brazier – stove

ACTIVITIES

1 Visualising the scene

Look at the illustration that accompanies the poem. Discuss in pairs or a small group how *you* visualise the scene. Make a list of the ways in which the illustration IS and IS NOT like the scene you imagine – for example, does Prince Kano look how you thought he would? And is the atmosphere right?

2 Rhythm and rhyme

> **Rhyming couplets**
> A style of poetry where one line rhymes with the line that comes straight after it. Look at the first two lines: notice how 'way' rhymes with 'day'. Then notice how the third and fourth lines rhyme, and so on.

The poem is written in rhyming couplets – one line rhymes with the one that follows it. It also has a quite strong sense of rhythm.

Explore the effect of the rhyme. Some readers might say that it makes the poem feel obvious and plodding. Others would argue that it gives it a feeling of mystery. How predictable is the rhyme scheme? Cover up the poem for a moment. Look at the lines opposite from the middle of the poem. The last word in each couplet has been left out. Can you predict what it is?

Half dead with fear the Prince
    staggered away,
Rushed blindly through the wood till break
    of _____;
And then he saw a larger clearing, filled
With houses, people, but his soul was
    _____;

Too easy? Try filling in both rhyming words in the couplets.

He looked around for comfort, and his
_____
Led him inside a small, half-empty
_____
Where monks prayed. 'Father,' to one he
_____,
'I've seen a dreadful thing; I am _____.'

This activity will probably show you that the rhymes in the poem are fairly predictable. Should this be a criticism of the poem? What effect would it have if the poem didn't rhyme at all, for example? Use the gaps above to experiment by placing words there that don't rhyme. Then write a paragraph about:

a your response to the current pattern of rhymes

b how the effect of the poem would be different if it did not rhyme.

Far Over the Misty Mountains

by J. R. R. Tolkien

You may know J. R. R. Tolkien through his novels *The Hobbit* and *Lord of the Rings*. If so, you will know that his characters come from a time long ago, when dwarves and goblins lived on Earth. This song is from *The Hobbit*. It is the song the dwarves sing to Bilbo Baggins, the hobbit.

Word Bank

ere – old word meaning before

enchanted – magic

yore – long ago

hoard – collection (e.g. treasure)

delves – digs

dale – valley

ire – anger

laid low – destroyed

Far Over the Misty Mountains

Far over the misty mountains cold
To dungeons deep and caverns old
We must away ere break of day
To seek the pale enchanted gold.

5   The dwarves of yore made mighty spells,
While hammers fell like ringing bells
In places deep, where dark things sleep,
In hollow halls beneath the fells.

For ancient king and elvish lord
10 There many a gleaming golden hoard
They shaped and wrought, and light they caught
To hide in gems on hilt of sword.

On silver necklaces they strung
The flowering stars, on crowns they hung
15 The dragon-fire, in twisted wire
They meshed the light of moon and sun.

Far over the misty mountains cold
To dungeons deep and caverns old
We must away, ere break of day,
20 To claim our long-forgotten gold.

Goblets they carved there for themselves
And harps of gold; where no man delves
There lay they long, and many a song
Was sung unheard by men or elves.

25 The pines were roaring on the height,
The winds were moaning in the night.
The fire was red, it flaming spread;
The trees like torches blazed with light.

The bells were ringing in the dale
30 And men looked up with faces pale;
The dragon's ire more fierce than fire
Laid low their towers and houses frail.

The mountains smoked beneath the moon;
The dwarves, they heard the tramp of doom.
35 They fled their hall to dying fall
Beneath his feet, beneath the moon.

Far over the misty mountains grim
To dungeons deep and caverns dim
We must away, ere break of day,
40 To win our harps and gold from him!

54

ACTIVITIES

1 Mood

Imagine the scene: a group of dwarves are singing this song to Bilbo Baggins.

a What is the song about?

b What does it say about the dragon?

c Is it a positive song or is there something menacing about it?

2 Language

The poem is set in an imaginary past. There are a number of ways that the writer gives it an ancient feel. One is the way he changes the word order, as in line 1:

Far over the misty mountains cold

In modern English we usually put the adjective in front of the thing it describes (the noun, <u>mountains</u>), like this:

Far over the cold misty mountains

Now take these other examples of word inversion and, again, write them in modern English:

a 'To <u>dungeons deep</u> and <u>caverns old</u>' (line 2)

b 'And men looked up with <u>faces pale</u>' (line 30)

c 'Laid low their <u>towers and houses frail</u>' (line 32 – you'll need to decide here whether it's the houses that are frail, or the houses and the towers)

d 'Far over the <u>misty mountains grim</u>' (line 37)

e 'To <u>dungeons deep</u> and <u>caverns dim</u>' (line 38)

> ### Adjectives and nouns
> Nouns are things – the words we use to label objects and ideas. Some nouns we can touch and see – <u>crowns</u>, <u>mountains</u>, <u>feet</u>; others are more abstract – <u>spells</u>, <u>sleep</u>, <u>doom</u>. Adjectives are words we use to describe nouns – <u>heavy crowns</u>, <u>misty mountains</u>, <u>aching feet</u>, <u>mighty spells</u>, <u>uneasy sleep</u>, <u>terrible doom</u>.

Replace J. R. R. Tolkein's word order with the updated version. Then try reading the poem aloud and discuss:

● how it changes the feel of the poem.

● whether the poem suddenly feels less 'old'

● whether it feels less mysterious.

3 Vocabulary

Here are some of the words that give the poem its mysterious, old-fashioned feel:

● goblets
● wrought
● delves
● dwarves
● ere
● yore
● ire.

> ### Synonyms
> Synonyms are words with similar meanings – for example, closed, shut, locked. The meaning of all of these words is not <u>exactly</u> the same: closing a car door is not the same as locking it. But the words are close enough in meaning that we would class them as synonyms.

Look at the words in the context of the poem to work out what each one means. Then decide whether you agree with the group's choice of words. Do they all seem old-fashioned words to you? Which two words feel oldest? Which two feel most recent?

Using your own ideas and, perhaps, a thesaurus, try to find synonyms for each word. For goblets, for example, you might think of: cups, mugs, glasses, beakers, tankards. Try each one out in the poem and talk about the effect it has. Does the poem suddenly seem more modern? Do some words fit well? Do some make the poem seem silly or childish?

Write a paragraph describing the effect of your vocabulary experiment.

The Survivors *by R. S. Thomas*

This poem has a gripping storyline – an adventure
out at sea with a disturbing, incomplete ending.

The Survivors

I never told you this.
He told me about it often:
Seven days in an open boat – burned out,
No time to get food:
5 Biscuits and water and the unwanted sun,
With only the oars' wing-beats for motion,
Labouring heavily towards land
That existed on a remembered chart,
Never on the horizon
10 Seven miles from the boat's bow.

After two days song dried on their lips;
After four days speech.
On the fifth cracks began to appear
In the faces' masks; salt scorched them.
15 They began to think about death,
Each man to himself, feeding it
On what the rest could not conceal.
The sea was as empty as the sky,
A vast disc under a dome
20 Of the same vastness, perilously blue.

But on the sixth day towards evening
A bird passed. No one slept that night;
The boat had become an ear
Straining for the desired thunder
25 Of the wrecked waves. It was dawn when it came,
Ominous as the big guns
Of enemy shores. The men cheered it.
From the swell's rise one of them saw the ruins
Of all that sea, where a lean horseman
30 Rode towards them and with a rope
Galloped them up on to the curt sand.

Word Bank

conceal – hide
perilously – dangerously
ominous – deeply disturbing
curt – short

ACTIVITIES

1 Narrative voices

The poem starts with a mystery. Who do you think 'I' is in the first line? Who do you think 'you' might be? And who could 'He' in line 2 be? With a partner, or in a small group, suggest some possible people.

2 The developing story

Look more closely at the way the story develops day by day. Use the prompts below to guide you.

a What happened to the ship that made the men abandon it?

b How can you tell that they had to evacuate it quickly?

c How can you tell that they didn't have time to bring a map with them?

d How do the men change after two, four and five days? The writer tells us something about their mood at each point.

e Why, on the sixth day, would no one sleep after seeing a bird?

f What happens to the men at the end?

3 Poetry/prose debate

Does the poem *feel* like a poem? Or does it read like prose (everyday language)? Here's what one reader says about it.

> The text reads a bit like a monologue, as if the survivor is talking to us about his experiences. It doesn't feel at all like a poem. There's no rhyme, no strong sense of rhythm. There aren't many images to make it feel poetic. It's a good storyline, but I don't think it's a poem.

Do you agree?

Look at the words the writer uses, the layout, any use of rhythm or rhyme, the way he leaves some details to the reader's imagination. Draw two columns on a piece of paper and list clues that show this is a poem, and clues to suggest that it is prose.

If you have easy access to a word processor, type out about eight lines of the poem as if it were a story. (Ignore the poet's original layout.) Then read it back. Does it feel 'odd' as prose? Does it feel as if it belongs in the form of a poem?

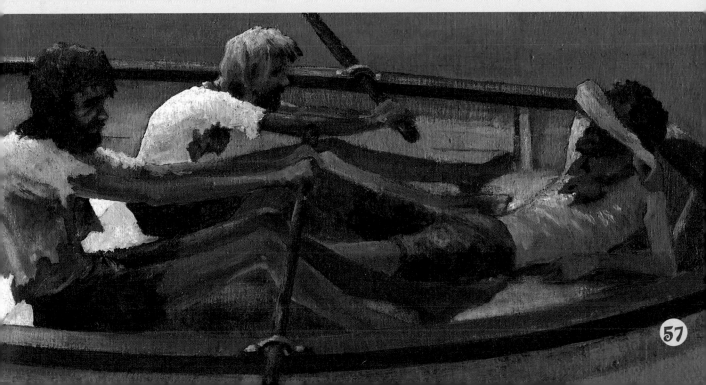

PRE-1900

The Way through the Woods *by Rudyard Kipling*

Rudyard Kipling was popular at the end of the last century for his poems and stories for children. He was author, for example, of the *Jungle Book,* later adapted (twice) as a film by Walt Disney. He also wrote poems about the First World War. This poem is about a place that has changed.

The Way through the Woods

They shut the road through the woods
    Seventy years ago.
Weather and rain have undone it again,
    And now you would never know
5 There was once a road through the woods
    Before they planted the trees.
It is underneath the coppice and heath,
    And the thin anemones.
    Only the keeper sees
10 That, where the ring-dove broods,
    And the badgers roll at ease,
There was once a road through the woods.

Yet, if you enter the woods
    Of a summer evening late,
15 When the night-air cools on the trout-ringed pools
    Where the otter whistles his mate,
(They fear not men in the woods,
    Because they see so few)
You will hear the beat of a horse's feet
20   And the swish of a skirt in the dew,
    Steadily cantering through
The misty solitudes,
    As though they perfectly knew
The old lost road through the woods. . . .
25 But there is no road through the woods.

Word Bank

coppice – woods

anemones – woodland flowers

cantering – riding at a steady pace

solitudes – lonely places

ACTIVITIES

1 Understanding

The woods are a place dominated by nature – for example, plants, badgers, otters. What signs are there in the poem that few humans ever come here?

2 Opinions

Here is a series of different comments about the poem. Use the comments to decide what your opinions are. For each one, say whether you agree, disagree or are not sure. Try to explain why.

Comment	Agree?	Disagree?	Not sure?	Opinion
The use of rhyme makes the poem move faster.				
The mysterious last line makes it similar to 'The Haunted Lift'.				
The writer uses very poetic vocabulary – such as 'misty solitudes' and 'a summer evening late'.				
This isn't really a mysterious poem – just a description.				
The rhythm makes you think of horses' hooves.				

3 Rhyme

The poem has a complex pattern of rhymes which help to create its haunting atmosphere. Like many poems, it has rhymes at the end of its lines. Find end-of-line rhymes for these words:

Verse 1

woods   _____

ago   _____

Verse 2

anemones   _____

Verse 3

few   _____

through   _____

The poem also uses something called internal rhyme. Look, for example, at line 3:

Weather and <u>rain</u> have undone it <u>again</u>

The poem contains three more examples of internal rhyme. See if you can find them. The best way is probably to read the poem aloud again and listen to the sounds.

Internal rhyme
We usually expect rhymes at the ends of the lines of poems. But sometimes poets use words in the middle of a line that rhyme with the word at the end, for example, <u>rain</u> and <u>again</u>. This adds to the complexity of the sound patterns in the text.

CLOSE READING

The Listeners *by Walter de la Mare*

This well-known poem continues to fascinate readers. It describes a journey, but gives us little detail about either its purpose or the identity of the traveller.

Word Bank

champed – chewed at

turret – tower

perplexed – confused

phantom – ghostly

thronging – filling

hearkening – listening

smote (old word) – knocked

The Listeners

'Is there anybody there?' said the Traveller,
  Knocking on the moonlit door;
And his horse in the silence champed the grasses
  Of the forest's ferny floor:
5 And a bird flew up out of the turret,
  Above the Traveller's head:
And he smote upon the door again a second time;
  'Is there anybody there?' he said.
But no one descended to the Traveller;
10 No head from the leaf-fringed sill
Leaned over and looked into his grey eyes,
  Where he stood perplexed and still.
But only a host of phantom listeners
  That dwelt in the lone house then
15 Stood listening in the quiet of the moonlight
  To that voice from the world of men:
Stood thronging the faint moonbeams on the dark stair,
  That goes down to the empty hall,
Hearkening in an air stirred and shaken
20 By the lonely Traveller's call.
And he felt in his heart their strangeness,
  Their stillness answering his cry,
While his horse moved, cropping the dark turf,
  'Neath the starred and leafy sky;
25 For he suddenly smote on the door, even
  Louder, and lifted his head:—
'Tell them I came, and no one answered,
  That I kept my word,' he said.
Never the least stir made the listeners,
30 Though every word he spake
Fell echoing through the shadowiness of the still house
From the one man left awake:
Ay, they heard his foot upon the stirrup,
  And the sound of iron on stone,
35 And how the silence surged softly backward,
  When the plunging hoofs were gone.

CLOSE READING

Advice on reading

This section develops your ability to respond to the language of a single poem. Start by reading the poem through once, perhaps jotting down notes about your first impressions. Then look at the questions below. What areas are you being asked to focus on? Now read the poem carefully once more, again making notes of ideas that occur to you. Remember that responding to an unseen poem will often require you to read it through carefully three or more times.

Advice on writing

Remember to answer each question in a full sentence or paragraph. Support your ideas with examples from the text wherever possible. Try to quote just a few words at a time rather than copying out chunks of the text.

Questions

Storyline

a Write a paragraph describing what we learn about the Traveller.

b What do you think the Traveller's purpose is?

c Do you think the listeners are ghosts or real people? How can you tell?

Style

d What do you notice about the use of rhythm and rhyme in the poem? Does it add to the mystery of the storyline? If so, try to explain how.

e The writer uses some old-fashioned words, such as <u>champed</u> and <u>smote</u>. Try to find two other examples of old-fashioned words. Describe the effect of these words in the poem.

f What do you like or dislike about the poem?

Focus on sound

Starting Points

Nursery rhymes, playground songs, nonsense verses and counting rhymes are part of our early language. The poems in this unit explore these powerful rhythms, rhymes and sound effects.

Three Limericks (Anonymous)

Limericks are poems that have a strong pattern of rhythm and rhyme, and which usually deal with very silly subject matter. People often love them or hate them.

More Limericks by 'Anonymous'

1

   There was an old person of Fratton
   Who would go to church with his hat on.
   'If I wake up,' he said,
   'With a hat on my head,
    5 I will know that it hasn't been sat on.'

2

   A man on the flying trapeze
   Emitted a terrible sneeze.
   The consequent force
   Shot him right off his course,
    5 And they found him next day in some trees.

3

   There was an old man of Peru
   Who dreamt he was eating his shoe.
   He woke in the night
   In a terrible fright,
    5 And found it was perfectly true.

ACTIVITIES

1 Speaking aloud

Working in pairs or small groups, practise reading these limericks aloud. You might try:

- reading them as fast as you can – perhaps having a race to see who can read most quickly

- each person reading a consecutive line

- each person reading a consecutive word (you have to practise to make this run smoothly!).

2 Limerick construction kit

Look again at the three limericks. How would you give instructions on writing a limerick to someone who had never seen or read one before? What are the essential ingredients? Write down your step-by-step construction kit. You should aim to give advice on:

- the number of lines

- rhythm

- rhyme

- subject matter.

Compare your notes with a partner's to see if you included all the essential points. You could then ask students in a different class to take your notes and follow them exactly. See if they end up writing a poem that counts as a limerick.

3 Write a limerick

Now write your own limerick. Start by thinking of a suitable subject matter – generally an unusual or eccentric person.

Some possible starting points might be:

- There was a young person called ...

- A man who was terribly ...

- A woman who bought a new ...

- A farmer with worrying ... .

You might have a class limerick competition. Draw each limerick out of a box, then read it aloud without saying who wrote it. Finally, take a vote on each one and decide on a winner.

Night Mail *by W. H. Auden*

W. H. Auden wrote hundreds of poems and liked to say that he had written in every possible poetry style. Certainly he wrote serious love poems, political poetry and lighter, comic verse. This poem is a narrative that captures not only the rhythm of the steam train era, but also the excitement we all feel at receiving our post. Auden wrote it to accompany a film made by the General Post Office about the way mail was transported overnight across the length of Britain.

Night Mail

I
This is the Night Mail crossing the Border,
Bringing the cheque and the postal order,

Letters for the rich, letters for the poor,
The shop at the corner, the girl next door.

5 Pulling up Beattock, a steady climb:
The gradient's against her, but she's on time.

Past cotton-grass and moorland boulder,
Shovelling white steam over her shoulder,

Snorting noisily, she passes
10 Silent miles of wind-bent grasses.

Birds turn their heads as she approaches,
Stare from bushes at her blank-faced coaches.

Sheep-dogs cannot turn her course;
They slumber on with paws across.

15 In the farm she passes no one wakes,
But a jug in a bedroom gently shakes.

II
Dawn freshens. Her climb is done.
Down towards Glasgow she descends,
Towards the steam tugs yelping down a glade of cranes,
20 Towards the fields of apparatus, the furnaces
Set on the dark plain like gigantic chessmen.
All Scotland waits for her:
In dark glens, beside pale-green lochs,
Men long for news.

III
25 Letters of thanks, letters from banks,
Letters of joy from girl and boy,
Receipted bills and invitations
To inspect new stock or to visit relations,
And applications for situations,
30 And timid lovers' declarations,
And gossip, gossip from all the nations,
News circumstantial, news financial,
Letters with holiday snaps to enlarge in,
Letters with faces scrawled on the margin,
35 Letters from uncles, cousins and aunts,
Letters to Scotland from the South of France,
Letters of condolence to Highlands and Lowlands,
Written on paper of every hue,
The pink, the violet, the white and the blue,
40 The chatty, the catty, the boring, the adoring,
The cold and official and the heart's outpouring,
Clever, stupid, short and long,
The typed and the printed and the spelt
   all wrong.

IV
Thousands are still asleep,
45 Dreaming of terrifying monsters
Or a friendly tea beside the band in Cranston's or Crawford's:
Asleep in working Glasgow, asleep in well-set Edinburgh,
Asleep in granite Aberdeen,
They continue their dreams,
50 But shall wake soon and hope for letters,
And none will hear the postman's knock
Without a quickening of the heart.
For who can bear to feel himself forgotten?

Word Bank

Beattock – a hill in Dumfriesshire, Scotland

gradient – slope

glens – Scottish word meaning valleys

lochs – lakes

circumstantial – personal

condolence – expressing sorrow at a death

hue – shade

ACTIVITIES

1 Structure: content

The poem is structured in four sections. How would you summarise the theme or content of these sections? Write one sentence about each of them.

2 Structure: style

Think about how each section differs. Use the questions below to help you.

a Which section has the strongest sense of rhythm? (Choose a line as an example.)

b Which has the strongest sense of rhyme? (Choose an example.)

c Where does the poem seem to speed up?

d Where does it seem to slow down?

e Which section do you think should be read quickest?

f Which section feels most like poetry?

g Which feels least like poetry? (Try to say why.)

3 Rhyme

a One of the most important ingredients in the poem is the use of rhythm and rhyme to create the sound of a locomotive. Look again at the first section. The writer uses rhyming couplets – pairs of lines that end with a rhyme.

How does this rhyme scheme create a feeling of the movement of a train? What would

Couplets and quatrains

These two words describe types of verses used in poetry. Just as in prose you would structure ideas in paragraphs, so poets often use verses (or stanzas). Couplets are pairs of lines – as in the first section of 'Night Mail'. If the two lines rhyme, they are called rhyming couplets. Quatrains are sets of four lines. They don't have to rhyme, but they usually do – line 2 and 4 rhyming and, sometimes, lines 1 and 3.

happen if the poem used quatrains – sequences of four lines with alternating rhymes – instead?

b Now look at section 3 of the poem. This uses some rhyming couplets, plus some internal rhyme. Internal rhyme is where a word in the middle of a line rhymes with the one at the end of the line – like this:

...............thanks..........banks (line 25)

See if you can find four more examples of internal rhyme from this section.

4 Rhythm

The poem also creates a powerful feeling of rhythm. Here are four descriptions of the use of rhythm in each section. Working in pairs or small groups, decide which description best matches each section.

a The rhythm here is the fastest of all – lots of short beats giving the impression of a train moving very quickly. It would be almost impossible to read this section slowly – the rhythm of all the syllables carries you along rapidly.

b The rhythm here is fast-moving. Short beats followed by a strong pulse, twice in every line, give a powerful feeling of a train moving through the countryside.

c The rhythm here feels least like poetry. It's slower and more reflective, without such an urgent sense of movement. This is the slowest pace of all the sections.

d The rhythm here feels gentler, less regular. It feels more like everyday conversation, someone telling us something, rather than a strongly poetic rhythm.

Compare your response with others in your class. Give reasons for your decisions.

Prayer Before Birth

by Louis MacNeice

This poem imagines a child's hopes and fears before it is born. The structure of the text allows the writer to create something that sounds like a charm or prayer. Start by thinking how you would read it aloud.

Word Bank

console – comfort

dandle – support

engendered – thought up

hector – preach at

humanity – the things that make me human

dragoon – force

lethal automaton – deadly machine

dissipate – dissolve

Prayer Before Birth

I am not yet born; O hear me.
Let not the bloodsucking bat or the rat or the stoat or the club-
    footed ghoul come near me.

I am not yet born, console me.
5 I fear that the human race may with tall walls wall me,
    with strong drugs dope me, with wise lies lure me,
    on black racks rack me, in blood-baths roll me.

I am not yet born; provide me
With water to dandle me, grass to grow for me, trees to talk
10   to me, sky to sing to me, birds and a white light
    in the back of my mind to guide me.

I am not yet born; forgive me
For the sins that in me the world shall commit, my words
    when they speak me, my thoughts when they think me,
15   my treason engendered by traitors beyond me,
    my life when they murder by means of my
    hands, my death when they live me.

I am not yet born; rehearse me
In the parts I must play and the cues I must take when
20   old men lecture me, bureaucrats hector me, mountains
    frown at me, lovers laugh at me, the white
    waves call me to folly and the desert calls
    me to doom and the beggar refuses
    my gift and my children curse me.

25 I am not yet born; O hear me,
Let not the man who is beast or who thinks he is God
    come near me.

I am not yet born; O fill me
With strength against those who would freeze my
30   humanity, would dragoon me into a lethal automaton,
    would make me a cog in a machine, a thing with
    one face, a thing, and against all those
    who would dissipate my entirety, would
    blow me like thistledown hither and
35   thither or hither and thither
    like water held in the
    hands would spill me.

Let them not make me a stone and let them not spill me.
Otherwise kill me.

ACTIVITIES

1 Techniques

The poem uses an amazing variety of techniques involving sounds. Fill in the 'Examples' column for each of the techniques listed below. Then try to match it up to the 'effect' statement that best describes how the technique works.

Techique	Examples	Effect
Each section of the poem builds up, gaining new lines.		This gives a feeling that everything in the text links together. It also adds to the sense of rhythm.
Repetition – e.g. 'I am not yet born'.		This adds to the pace of the poem. We don't have to wait to the end of lines for rhymes; instead we hear them throughout, making the text sound more unusual and haunting.
Use of alliteration – thoughts/think; traitors/treason. The writer uses internal rhyme – e.g. bat/rat; tall/walls; wise/lies.		This technique gives the child's prayer more power because it emphasises the emotions. It brings the fears to life. This reinforces the message of the poem and emphasises the feelings of the child.
The writer uses emotive words with powerful emotional associations – traitors, curse, beast.		This technique gives the poem a powerful sense of momentum – of moving forward. The poem actually seems to get faster because of this technique.

2 Sounds

This poem sounds wonderful when read aloud dramatically. It works well if you can:

- vary the pace at which you read it
- use different voices for different lines
- whisper some parts; speak others all at the same time; shout some
- emphasise the sounds of the words and let your listener feel the rhythm of the text.

Work in pairs or small groups and put together a lively, dramatic reading. You might record it onto tape, then play it back to the class, so that they focus entirely on the sounds and not on the sight of you performing it.

3 Personal response

One reader says: 'This is an example of a poem where the style is far more important than the content. You can enjoy and admire the way it is written without really understanding what it is about.'

Do you agree? Discuss in groups.

Woman Work *by Maya Angelou*

This poem has a different feel to others in this unit. It is a text with a strong but simple message, and the repetition throughout the poem makes this message all the more powerful.

Woman Work

I've got the children to tend
The clothes to mend
The floor to mop
The food to shop
5 Then the chicken to fry
The baby to dry
I got company to feed
The garden to weed
I've got the shirts to press
10 The tots to dress
The cane to be cut
I gotta clean up this hut
Then see about the sick
And the cotton to pick.

15 Shine on me, sunshine
Rain on me, rain
Fall softly, dewdrops
And cool my brow again.

Storm, blow me from here
20 With your fiercest wind
Let me float across the sky
'Til I can rest again.

Fall gently, snowflakes
Cover me with white
25 Cold icy kisses and
Let me rest tonight.

Sun, rain, curving sky
Mountain, oceans, leaf and stone
Star shine, moon glow
30 You're all that I can call my own.

ACTIVITIES

1 Narrative voice

What impression do you get of the narrator of the poem?

- What is she like?
- Where does she live?
- What do you know about her children?
- What are her feelings about her life?

Using the answers to these questions, make some notes on her.

2 Rhythm

The poem works through a series of lists. Look at lines 1–2 as an example.

I've got the children to tend
The clothes to mend

The rhythm here is created through rhyming couplets (to revise these, see page 65). Then suddenly, in line 15, the speaker changes the rhythm and says:

Shine on me, sunshine

The writer suddenly uses quatrains with an ABCB rhyme scheme.

Look at the subject matter of the poem and think about why the rhythm and rhyme change at this point. What effect does the change of style have?

3 Vocabulary

Just as the rhythm and rhyme scheme change halfway through the poem, so does the vocabulary. The first part uses mostly concrete nouns; the second part uses mostly abstract nouns.

Concrete and abstract nouns

Nouns are the words that we use to label things. Concrete nouns refer to things we can usually touch or which exist in the real world – potato, desk, clock. Abstract nouns refer to concepts and feelings – thing we cannot touch – hope, work, time, winter, love.

Using the language panel to help you, look at the following words from the poem and decide whether you think they are concrete or abstract. For the moment, try not to look back at the poem to help you.

Words	Concrete (C) or abstract (A)?
chicken	
sun	
white	
floor	
tots	
tonight	
moon	
baby	

Now look at the vocabulary of the poem again. Why do you think the writer tends to use concrete words in the first part and abstract words in the second part? How does this use of vocabulary emphasise the message of her poem? This isn't easy – so spend some time talking through your answer.

Tarantella *by Hilaire Belloc*

A tarantella is an energetic dance from Taranto in Southern Italy, and Hilaire Belloc uses some of the swirling rhythms of the dance to create this lively poem. As you read it, notice how the rhythms change and develop, and the picture you get of the main character, Miranda. The poem is also something of a mystery, so see if you can work out what has happened.

Tarantella

1 Do you remember an Inn,
2 Miranda?
3 Do you remember an Inn?
4 And the tedding and the spreading
5 Of the straw for a bedding,
6 And the fleas that tease in the High Pyrenees,
7 And the wine that tasted of the tar?
8 And the cheers and the jeers of the young muleteers
9 (Under the vine of the dark verandah)?
10 Do you remember an Inn, Miranda,
11 Do you remember an Inn?
12 And the cheers and the jeers of the young muleteers
13 Who hadn't got a penny,
14 And who weren't paying any,
15 And the hammer at the doors and the Din?
16 And the Hip! Hop! Hap!
17 Of the clap
18 Of the hands to the twirl and the swirl
19 Of the girl gone chancing,
20 Glancing,
21 Dancing,
22 Backing and advancing,
23 Snapping of the clapper to the spin
24 Out and in———
25 And the Ting, Tong, Tang of the Guitar!
26 Do you remember an Inn,
27 Miranda?
28 Do you remember an Inn?
29 Never more ;
30 Miranda,
31 Never more.
32 Only the high peaks hoar :
33 And Aragon a torrent at the door.
34 No sound
35 In the walls of the Halls were falls
36 The tread
37 Of the feet of the dead to the ground
38 No sound :
39 But the boom
40 Of the far Waterfall like Doom.

Word Bank

muleteers – men who look after the donkeys

hoar – frosty, white

Aragon – river in north-east Spain

Doom – death, fate

ACTIVITIES

1 Understanding

This is a strange and haunting poem. Start by working in small groups to see what you think it is about. Use the questions below to help focus your discussions.

a Who is Miranda?

b Who is the person speaking to her?

c What was their relationship?

d Why were they dancing?

e Why do you think the dancing ended?

f Why do you think the tone of the last section of the poem is so different?

2 Structure

The poem has a lively, fast-moving style, which sometimes changes. Working with a partner, look more closely at the way the text develops. You'll see that the lines have been numbered 1–40. Write these numbers down in a list. Then, reading the poem through aloud, group them together to show lines that have a similar style. Against each set of lines, write down what you notice. You might say:

- these move quickly
- the rhythm is very fast
- the speed slows down here
- the rhyme stops
- the writer repeats the same word
- the sentences change into questions
- the narrator sounds happy ... depressed ... confused.

3 Sounds revision

'Tarantella' uses many of the sound techniques we have encountered in earlier poems. Use the poem to revise your knowledge of these different techniques. See if you can find an example of each of the following:

- a rhyming couplet
- line-end rhyme
- internal rhyme
- alliteration
- onomatopoeia.

Use the glossary on pages 124–7 to check definitions if you need to.

4 Response

What do you make of the poem? Do you like it or do you think it's daft? Does it mean anything or is it chiefly a collection of poetic techniques? Discuss or write a paragraph about your response.

CLOSE READING

PRE-1900

Feste's Song *by William Shakespeare*

Twelfth Night is one of Shakespeare's most bitter-sweet comedies – very funny, but based on some cruel and upsetting humour. The play ends with this song by the clown, Feste, who looks back over his own life.

Feste's Song

FESTE (*Sings*)

When that I was and a little tiny boy,
  With hey, ho, the wind and the rain;
A foolish thing was but a toy,
  For the rain it raineth every day.

5 But when I came to man's estate,
  With hey, ho, the wind and the rain;
'Gainst knaves and thieves men shut their gate,
  For the rain it raineth every day.

But when I came, alas, to wive,
10 With hey, ho, the wind and the rain;
By swaggering could I never thrive,
  For the rain it raineth every day.

But when I came unto my beds,
  With hey, ho, the wind and the rain;
15 With toss-pots still had drunken heads,
  For the rain it raineth every day.

A great while ago the world begun,
  With hey, ho, the wind and the rain;
But that's all one, our play is done,
20 And we'll strive to please you every day.

Word Bank

man's estate – adulthood

knaves – villains

wive – marry

toss-pots – drunkards

CLOSE READING

Advice on reading

This section develops your ability to respond to the language of a single poem. Start by reading the poem through once, perhaps jotting down notes about your first impressions. Then look at the questions below. What areas are you being asked to focus on? Now read the poem carefully once more, again making notes of ideas that occur to you. Remember that responding to an unseen poem will often require you to read it through carefully three or more times.

Advice on writing

Remember to answer each question in a full sentence or paragraph. Support your ideas with examples from the text wherever possible. Try to quote just a few words at a time rather than copying out chunks of the text.

Questions

a How can you tell that the song is taken from a play?

b The song tells a kind of story. Say in a sentence or two what it describes.

c The poem is written in quatrains with an ABAC rhyme scheme. Say in your own words what this means.

d What different kinds of repetition do you notice in the poem?

e What clues are there that the text was written before this century?

f What do you think of the song? Write a few sentences describing your response.

Focus on image

Starting Points

Images are the pictures words create in our minds. The poems in this unit use images to create vivid impressions of people and places.

A Martian Sends a Postcard Home

by Craig Raine

Craig Raine's poem is a puzzle. Imagine an alien creature landing on Earth and seeing things for the very first time. Imagine not knowing what things are or what they do. See if you can work out from the Martian's descriptions what the main objects are.

A Martian Sends a Postcard Home

(A)
Caxtons are mechanical birds with many wings
and some are treasured for their markings –
they cause the eyes to melt
or the body to shriek without pain.
I have never seen one fly, but
sometimes they perch on the hand.

Mist is when the sky is tired of flight
and rests its soft machine on ground:
then the world is dim and bookish
like engravings under tissue paper.

Rain is when the earth is television.
It has the property of making colours darker.

(B)
Model T is a room with the lock inside –
a key is turned to free the world
for movement, so quick there is a film
to watch for anything missed.

But time is tied to the wrist
or kept in a box, ticking with impatience.

(C)
In homes, a haunted apparatus sleeps,
that snores when you pick it up.
If the ghost cries, they carry it
to their lips and soothe it to sleep
with sounds. And yet, they wake it up
deliberately, by tickling with a finger.

(D)
Only the young are allowed to suffer
openly. Adults go to a punishment room
with water but nothing to eat.
They lock the door and suffer the noises
alone. No one is exempt
and everyone's pain has a different smell.

(E)
At night, when all the colours die,
they hide in pairs
and read about themselves –
in colour, with their eyelids shut.

Word Bank

Caxton – inventor of the printing press

exempt – free from

ACTIVITIES

1 Image spotting

In pairs or small groups, try to work out what the five objects A, B, C, D and E are. If you get stuck, use the clues at the foot of this page.

2 Other images

Now look more closely at the way Craig Raine creates his images. Remember that an image is often made when a writer compares one thing with another. Explore how these images work by studying some of the examples below and using the annotations.

> *Imagery*
>
> Imagery is the word we use for a series of images. An image is a picture we see in our minds. Writers create images using three main techniques.
>
> 1 **Simile**: one thing is compared with another using the linking word as or like – for example, fast as lightning; leapt like a fox.
> 2 **Metaphor**: one thing is compared with another but without use of the linking word as or like – for example, He was a tiger in battle; Rain is when the earth is television.
> 3 **Personification**: an abstract concept (like time, death, hope) is presented as if it was a person or animal – for example, Death stalked the battlefields; Winter had claimed the world again.

A

Soft machine — hard to image for mist — does this image work for you?

Mist is when the sky is tired of flight and rests its soft machine on ground:

Why tired of flight? What picture do you see?

then the world is dim and bookish like engravings under tissue paper.

What image do you get from bookish? What picture does this create?

B

Does television do this?

Rain is when the earth is television. It has the property of making colours darker.

Can you see a connection between rain and television? When might a television screen look like rain?

C

But time is tied to the wrist or kept in a box, ticking with impatience

This image uses personification. How does the writer make time seem as if it is a person or animal?

Which of the images, A, B or C, do you find most successful? Which one works least well for you? Try to say why.

Clues

1 None of the answers is alive – they're all objects.
2 A is something you almost certainly have in your classroom.
3 C is definitely not alive.

If all else fails, you can look up the answers on page 128.

Windy Boy in a Windswept Tree

by Geoffrey Summerfield

Everyone knows how exciting and dramatic a powerful storm can be. Geoffrey Summerfield's poem describes the effect of a strong wind on a boy caught in a tree. His use of language helps us to see the scene in our minds.

Word Bank

smithereens – small pieces

capering – jumping wildly

Windy Boy in a Windswept Tree

The branch swayed, swerved,
Swept and whipped, up,
Down, right to left,
Then leapt to right again,
5 As if to hurl him down
To smash to smithereens
On the knife-edge grass
Or smother
In the close-knit quilts of moss.
10 Out on a crazy limb
He screwed his eyes tight shut,
To keep out the dizzy ground.
Sweat greased his palms;
Fear pricked his forehead.
15 The twisted branches lunged and lurched,
His body curved, twisted, he arched
His legs and gripped the bark

Between his ankles.
The crust of bark
20 Sharp as glasspaper
And rough with wrinkles
Grazed his skin
And raised the raw red flesh
And crazed his mind
25 With fears of breaking.
Then the mad-cap, capering wind
Dropped.
The branch steadied,
Paused,
30 Rested.
He slowly clambered, slowly back,
Slowly so safely,
Then dropped
Like a wet blanket
35 To the rick-like, reassuring ground.
Finally, without a sound
He walked carefully
Home.

ACTIVITIES

1 Character

The boy finally drops to the ground, 'Like a wet blanket' (line 34) and walks home 'without a sound' (line 36). Write a paragraph describing the thoughts in his head, thinking back to the experience in the tree and how he feels now. Use first person mode: 'I ...'

2 Verb study

One of the reasons the poem shows the power of the wind so well is the writer's choice of verbs to describe what it does. Look at the list below and, working on your own or with a partner, discuss which verb is the most active – the one that seems to create the strongest sense of force and power. Then decide which verb is the least active. Place all ten verbs in order – most active to least active – and compare your decisions with other people in your class.

- swayed
- swerved
- swept
- whipped
- leapt
- hurl
- smash
- smother
- lunged
- lurched

3 Bringing the wind to life

Geoffrey Summerfield uses personification to make the wind seem as if it is alive. Some words show the movement of the tree – such as 'swayed' and 'swerved'. Others make the tree sound like a human being – 'leapt to right again, / As if to hurl him down' (lines 4–5). The tree often sounds as if it is deliberately attacking the boy.

a Look through the poem and find some examples of where the wind seems to behave as if it is alive.

b Think about why the writer uses this technique. Which of the following reasons is most likely?

- Personifying the wind makes his poem more interesting.
- It makes the boy seem like a victim.
- It makes the wind seem aggressive.
- It helps us to imagine the power of the wind.
- It adds humour to the poem.

4 Other techniques

Here are some other techniques the writer uses to create a powerful impression. For each one, work on your own or with a partner to explain what effect you think the technique has.

Technique	Examples	Effect
alliteration	• swayed, swerved, swept • raised the raw red flesh	
simile	• sharp as glasspaper • like a wet blanket	
metaphor	• the knife-edge grass • quilts of moss • the crust of bark	

The Sea *by James Reeves*

This poem shows brilliantly how writers can bring scenes to life with a variety of techniques. It's a poem about the sea – but look how James Reeves gives the sea a life of its own, even a personality.

The Sea

The sea is a hungry dog,
Giant and grey.
He rolls on the beach all day.
With his clashing teeth and shaggy jaws
5 Hour upon hour he gnaws
The rumbling, tumbling stones,
And 'Bones, bones, bones, bones !'
The giant sea-dog moans,
Licking his greasy paws.

10 And when the night wind roars
And the moon rocks in the stormy cloud,
He bounds to his feet and snuffs and sniffs,
Shaking his wet sides over the cliffs,
And howls and hollos long and loud.

15 But on quiet days in May or June,
When even the grasses on the dune
Play no more their reedy tune,
With his head between his paws
He lies on the sandy shores,
20 So quiet, so quiet, he scarcely snores.

Word Bank

dune – area behind the beach where grasses grow amid the sand

ACTIVITIES

1 Bringing the sea to life

The main technique that James Reeves uses to bring the sea to life is personification (see 'Windy Boy in a Windswept Tree' on pages 76–77 to learn more about this). He makes the sea seem as if it is a person, or in this case a creature. His opening line sets the tone:

The sea is a hungry dog

a Look through the poem and find four examples that make the sea feel like a dog.

b Try to describe what effect this has – what impression of the sea it gives.

Describing the sea as if it was a dog makes it seem ...

2 Images

James Reeves uses some powerful visual images to create pictures in the reader's mind. Look at the examples below and describe the pictures they create for you.

a With his clashing teeth and shaggy jaws
(line 4)

b Hour upon hour he gnaws
The rumbling, tumbling stones
(lines 5–6)

c And the moon rocks in the stormy cloud
(line 11)

3 Other possibilities

James Reeves compares the sea to a dog. But what if he had chosen a different animal – say, a cat or a dragon? Try writing the first 6 lines of a poem that compares the sea to a different creature. Start with a similar opening line: 'The sea is a ...', giving your own choice of creature (for example, playful cat or angry dragon).

In the Nursery *by Anne Stevenson*

Anne Stevenson's poem has a simple event at its heart: she lifts a child from a crib and looks at him. That's all that happens. But her use of language transforms the moment into something much more special. Look at the way poetry can help us to see something extraordinary in everyday events.

In the Nursery

I lift the seven months baby from his crib,
a clump of roots.
Sleep drops off him like soil
in clods that smell sunbaked and rich with urine.
5 He opens his eyes,
two light blue corollas.
His cheek against mine
is the first soft day in the garden.
His mouth makes a bud, then a petal,
10 then a leaf.
In less than seven seconds
he's blossoming in a bowl of arms.

Word Bank

corollas – petals of a flower

ACTIVITIES

1 Understanding

What do you think is happening in this poem? Look at the descriptions below and decide which one you think best describes what the poem is about.

a It describes a baby waking up.

b It describes a mother looking at her child.

c It shows how contact between the mother and child brings them both to life.

d It describes the love a mother feels for her child.

e It describes the way a baby changes as he wakes up.

Perhaps none of these descriptions really gets to the heart of the poem. If not, write a sentence of your own which describes it better.

2 Imagery

When there is more than one image or picture in a poem, we call it imagery. Anne Stevenson's poem uses imagery from nature to show us something about the child and his mother. Look at some of the images and try to describe the picture they create in your mind.

Image	Picture in your mind
… a clump of roots	
Sleep drops off him like soil	
His cheek against mine is the first soft day in the garden	
he's blossoming in a bowl of arms	

3 Comparison

Some people love this poem. For others it doesn't have much effect. The idea of comparing a child to a plant might seem odd, but look more closely at the similarities Anne Stevenson suggests. Children and plants may have more in common than you think.

a Fill in the gaps where you can, either with notes or a few words from the poem, to show the connection between the two ideas.

Humans	Plants
	can be grown in a nursery
safe in a crib	
	rich smells of soil, fertiliser, etc.
soft skin	
shape of mouth	
	grows when cared for

b Now you have looked closely at the poem, what is your opinion of it? What do you like or dislike about it? Write a paragraph or two giving your own response.

An Ordinary Day
by *Norman MacCaig*

Norman MacCaig's poem reminds us of the creative power we have inside our minds. Faster and better than the world's most advanced computers, our brains can do almost anything. His poem shows how a creative mind can make the ordinary seem extraordinary.

An Ordinary Day

I took my mind a walk
Or my mind took me a walk—
Whichever was the truth of it.

The light glittered on the water
5   Or the water glittered in the light.
Cormorants stood on a tidal rock

With their wings spread out,
Stopping no traffic. Various ducks
Shilly-shallied here and there

10   On the shilly-shallying water.
An occasional gull yelped. Small flowers
Were doing their level best

To bring to their kerb bees like
Aerial charabancs. Long weeds in the clear
15   Water did Eastern dances, unregarded

By shoals of darning needles. A cow
Started a moo but thought
Better of it. . . . And my feet took me home

And my mind observed to me,
20   Or I to it, how ordinary
Extraordinary things are or

How extraordinary ordinary
Things are, like the nature of the mind
And the process of observing.

Word Bank

cormorants – large sea-birds

shilly-shallied – messing around

aerial – belonging in the air

charabancs – old-fashioned word for buses

unregarded – unnoticed

ACTIVITIES

1 Imagining the images

If you were being asked to provide an illustration for this poem, what would you do? Working on your own or in a pair, decide what kind of illustration you might have produced.

> **Stream of consciousness**
> Usually in writing we structure our ideas into an orderly sequence and use sentences and paragraphs to help the reader to follow what we mean. Stream of consciousness means allowing one idea to follow another in an unstructured way. It feels closer to the way we dream than the way we usually write.

2 Untangling images

Look at the two images below. Explain what you think they might mean, using some of the prompts provided.

Image	What it might mean
1 Small flowers Were doing their level best To bring to their kerb bees like Aerial charabancs ...	Why 'kerb'? What picture do you get of 'Aerial charabancs'?
2 shoals of darning needles	What is the writer describing here? What picture does it create?

3 Vocabulary

Part of the fascination of this poem is the way the writer puts unexpected words together. In pairs or small groups, explore some of the associations of words a little more – what they first make you think of. Write down the kinds of word that spring to mind. The first example is done for you.

Image	Word(s) you'd expect
I took my _____ a walk	dog suggests going for fresh air – seeing new sights – exploring
Various ducks _____ here and there	
An occasional ____ yelped	
Unregarded by shoals of _____	

CLOSE READING

Gold *by Ferenc Juhasz*

This poem comes from Hungary and was translated into English by Edwin Morgan and David Wevill. In it, a woman is feeding soup and bread to some children. Look at the way the writer presents the scene with powerful visual images. Read the text through several times before you answer the questions.

Gold

The woman touches her burr
of thinning hair. She laughs,
and drops a spoon and a hunk of bread
in their reaching, grubby hands.
5   Like roses divining water
the circle of thin red necks
leans over the steaming plates;
red noses bloom in the savoury mist.

The stars of their eyes shine
10   like ten worlds lost in their own light.
In the soup, slowly circling
swim golden onion rings.

CLOSE READING

Advice on reading

This section develops your ability to respond to the language of a single poem. Start by reading the poem through once, perhaps jotting down notes about your first impressions. Then look at the questions below. What areas are you being asked to focus on? Now read the poem carefully once more, again making notes of ideas that occur to you. Remember that responding to an unseen poem will often require you to read it through carefully three or more times.

Advice on writing

Remember to answer each question in a full sentence or paragraph. Support your ideas with examples from the text wherever possible. Try to quote just a few words at a time rather than copying out chunks of the text.

Questions

a Look at the first 5 lines. What impression do you get of the woman? How old is she? How is she feeling? How does she behave towards the children?

b Now look at the rest of the poem. What impression do you get of the children? Why might their hands be grubby and their noses red? How can you tell that they are hungry?

c What picture do you see in the image 'red noses bloom in the savoury mist'?

d What do you think the writer might mean by 'The stars of their eyes shine / like ten worlds lost in their own light' (lines 9–10)? Try to explain the image in your own words.

e Why do you think the writer has called the poem 'Gold'?

f Do you like the poem? Explain why or why not.

Narrative poems

Starting Points

A narrative poem tells a story. This unit explores narrative poems old and new – in particular how they can be used to structure stories, create atmosphere and build tension.

A Case of Murder *by Vernon Scannell*

This is an unpleasant tale of cruelty. It starts as a realistic story and becomes something more menacing. As you read it, think about why the writer might have chosen to use poetry to tell his tale.

A Case of Murder

They should not have left him there alone,
Alone that is except for the cat.
He was only nine, not old enough
To be left alone in a basement flat,
5 Alone, that is, except for the cat.
A dog would have been a different thing,
A big gruff dog with slashing jaws,
But a cat with round eyes mad as gold,
Plump as a cushion with tucked-in paws –
10 Better have left him with a fair-sized rat!
But what they did was leave him with a cat.
He hated that cat ; he watched it sit,
A buzzing machine of soft black stuff,
He sat and watched and he hated it,
15 Snug in its fur, hot blood in a muff,
And its mad gold stare and the way it sat
Crooning dark warmth : he loathed all that.
So he took Daddy's stick and he hit the cat.
Then quick as a sudden crack in glass
20 It hissed, black flash, to a hiding place
In the dust and dark beneath the couch,
And he followed the grin on his new-made face,
A wide-eyed, frightened snarl of a grin,
And he took the stick and he thrust it in,

25 Hard and quick in the furry dark,
The black fur squealed and he felt his skin
Prickle with sparks of dry delight.
Then the cat again came into sight,
Shot for the door that wasn't quite shut,
30 But the boy, quick too, slammed fast the door :
The cat, half-through, was cracked like a nut
And the soft black thud was dumped on the floor.
Then the boy was suddenly terrified
And he bit his knuckles and cried and cried ;
35 But he had to do something with the dead thing there.
His eyes squeezed beads of salty prayer
But the wound of fear gaped wide and raw ;
He dared not touch the thing with his hands
So he fetched a spade and shovelled it
40 And dumped the load of heavy fur
In the spidery cupboard under the stair
Where it's been for years, and though it died
It's grown in that cupboard and its hot low purr
Grows slowly louder year by year :
45 There'll not be a corner for the boy to hide
When the cupboard swells and all sides split
And the huge black cat pads out of it.

Word Bank

crooning – singing softly

ACTIVITIES

1 Character

What does the poem tell us about the boy – his age, background, feelings? Make a list of character points based on what we learn about him throughout the whole poem (beginning, middle and end). Use a spider diagram for each, like this:

boy

2 Images

How does Vernon Scannell make the cat seem menacing? Look at the images below and comment on the picture they create of the cat. The first example is done for you.

Image	Comment
a cat with round eyes mad as gold (line 8)	'Round eyes' suggest that the cat keeps watching the boy. 'Mad as gold' tells us about the colour of the cat's eyes, but also hints that it is insane or perhaps just very unpredictable.
A buzzing machine of soft black stuff (line 13)	
Snug in its fur, hot blood in a muff (line 15)	
... the way it sat / Crooning dark warmth (line 16–17)	
It hissed, black flash, to a hiding place (line 20)	

Symbolism
We are surrounded by symbols – a green light on a traffic light means go. A plastic poppy in November symbolises the sacrifice of soldiers in war. A crucifix symbolises Christian faith. In literature, writers use symbolism to show a layer of meaning beneath the surface. At the end of this poem, for example, a black cat has become more than ordinary. To the boy it seems to symbolise something much more terrifying.

3 Symbolism

At first the poem seems like a straightforward story. By the end it has become symbolic – the image of 'the huge black cat' that comes out of the cupboard is probably not a real one. Perhaps it is part of the boy's imagination.

In a group, use some of the notes opposite to discuss what you think the cat at the end of the poem might symbolise. You may not agree with the view expressed in these notes. Feel free to reject it. But the notes should help you to reach a number of ideas about the possibilities at the end. Compare your ideas with others in your class.

The boy seems young early on – 'Daddy' Grows up too quickly?
Sexual images show him scared and out of his depth.
Lashes out and then regrets it.
No one to help him discuss his feelings.
Worries about cat – image of it festers in his mind.
Cat at the end symbolises the boy's ...

The Lake *by Roger McGough*

Poets sometimes use poetry to tackle important social issues. In the eighteenth century, writers would use verse to make fun of the politicians of the day. Poetry has also been used to communicate the personal horror of war. Nowadays, some poets write about politics or education or the environment, as this poem by Roger McGough shows. It presents a chilling vision of the effects of pollution.

Word Bank

sedge – marsh reeds

debris – rubbish

excreta – human waste, sewage

bemoan – complain about

acquired – gained

The Lake

For years there have been no fish in the lake.
People hurrying through the park avoid it
like the plague. Birds steer clear
and the sedge of course has withered.
5 Trees lean away from it,
and at night it reflects, not the moon,
but the blackness of its own depths.
There are no fish in the lake.
But there is life there. There is life . . .

10 Underwater pigs glide between reefs of coral debris.
They love it here. They breed and multiply
in sties hollowed out of the mud
and lined with mattresses and bedsprings.
They live on dead fish and rotting things,
15 drowned pets, plastic and assorted excreta.
Rusty cans they like the best.
Holding them in webbed trotters
their teeth tear easily through the tin,
and poking in a snout, they noisily suck out
20 the putrid matter within.

There are no fish in the lake.
But there is life there. There is life . . .

For on certain evenings after dark
shoals of pigs surface
25 and look out at those houses near the park.
Where, in bathrooms,
children feed stale bread to plastic ducks,
and in attics,
toy yachts have long since runaground.

30 Where, in livingrooms,
anglers dangle their lines on patterned carpets,
and bemoan the fate of the ones that got away.

Down on the lake, piggy eyes glisten.
They have acquired a taste for flesh.
They are licking their lips. Listen . . .

ACTIVITIES

1 Opinions

In small groups discuss what you think the poem is about. Use the opinions below to get started – try putting them in order of the one you most agree with to the one you least agree with. Use evidence from the text to support your points of view.

a The poem is a fantasy about the future.

b The poem is a piece of lighthearted entertainment; it hasn't any serious point.

c The poem is a warning about pollution.

d The poem describes how humans have lost control of the planet.

e The poem shows anger about the way nature is being destroyed.

2 Narrative structure

The poem is less obviously a narrative than some of the other texts in this unit. But it shows a clear development – what the lake used to be like, what it is like now, and a few hints about the future. Use the table below to explore the narrative structure in more detail.

3 Poetry ingredients

Based on what you have learnt from this book so far, you know that poetry can have a huge range of ingredients, including:

- patterned language
- images
- words with associations
- rhythm
- different types of rhyme
- meanings beneath the surface
- symbolism.

Which of these does 'The Lake' have? Some readers feel that it's actually a prose narrative set out like a poem. What do you think? Working in small groups, put together the arguments for and against the text being classified as a poem. Follow this with a discussion or debate, using as many examples from the poem as you can to see what conclusions you reach.

Past	Present	Future
• What did the lake used to be like? • What hints are there about the way people, birds and trees probably used to respond to the lake? • Look at the details of the toy yachts and fishing lines – what is the writer showing us about the past life of the lake?	• How do people view the lake now? Have they forgotten it – or do they try to ignore it altogether? • What is the lake like? • How are the pigs taking control of the lake?	• The ending feels quite menacing. Look again at the last three lines – what hints are there here about the future?

PRE-1900

Gelert, Llewelyn's Dog *by W. R. Spencer*

This eighteenth-century poem from Wales tells of a terrible misunderstanding
– a story that has become a fable in North Wales, where there is a village
called Beddgelert (or 'Gelert's grave') in memory of the events that took place.

Gelert, Llewelyn's Dog

The spearmen heard the bugle sound,
And cheerily smiled the morn.
And many a brach and many a hound
Attend Llewelyn's horn.

5 And still he blew a louder blast,
And gave a louder cheer –
Come Gelert! Why art thou the last
Llewelyn's horn to hear?

Oh where does faithful Gelert roam?
10 The flower of his race!
So true so brave! a lamb at home,
A lion in the chase.

'Twas only at Llewelyn's board
The faithful Gelert fed.
15 He watched, he served, he cheered his lord,
And sentinel'd his bed.

In sooth he was a peerless hound,
The gift of Royal John –
But now no Gelert could be found,
20 And all the chase rode on.

And now as over rocks and dells
The gallant chidings rise,
All Snowdon's craggy chaos yells
With many mingled cries.

25 That day Llewelyn little moved
The chase of hart or hare,
And scant and small the booty proved
For Gelert was not there.

Unpleased Llewelyn homeward hied.
30 When near the portal seat,
His truant, Gelert, he espied,
Bounding his lord to greet.

But when he gained his castle door,
Aghast the chieftain stood,
35 The hound all o'er was smeared with gore,
His lips, his fangs, ran blood.

Llewelyn gazed with wild surprise
Unused such looks to meet,
His favourite checked his joyful guise
40 And crouched and licked his feet.

Onward in haste Llewelyn passed –
And on went Gelert too –
And still where'er his eyes were cast
Fresh blood-gouts shocked his view.

45 O'erturned his infant's bed he found!
The blood-stained covert rent,
And all around the walls and ground,
With recent blood besprent!

He called his child – no voice replied!
50 He searched with terror wild.
Blood, blood, he found on every side!
But nowhere found his child!

Hell hound! my child's by thee devoured
The frantic father cried.
55 And to the hilt his vengeful sword
He plunged in Gelert's side.

His suppliant look, as to earth he fell,
No pity could impart,
But still his Gelert's dying yell
60 Past heavy o'er his heart.

Aroused by Gelert's dying yell
Some slumberer wakened nigh,
What words the parent's joy can tell
To hear his infant cry.

65 Concealed beneath a mangled heap
His hurried search had missed,
All glowing from his rosy sleep
His cherub boy he kissed!

Nor scratch had he, nor harm nor dread
70 But the same couch beneath
Lay a great wolf, all torn and dead –
Tremendous still in death.

Ah! what was then Llewelyn's pain
For now the truth was clear;
75 The gallant hound the wolf had slain
To save Llewelyn's heir.

Vain, vain was all of Llewelyn's woe
Best of all thy kind, adieu!
The frantic deed which had laid thee low
80 This heart shall ever rue!

And now a gallant tomb they raise
With costly sculpture decked,
And marbles storied with his praise
Poor Gelert's bones protect.

85 Here never could a spearman pass,
Or forester, unmoved.
Here oft the tear-besprinkled grass
Llewelyn's sorrow proved.

And here he hung his horn and spear
90 And oft as evening fell,
In fancy's piercing sounds would hear
Poor Gelert's dying yell.

Word Bank

spearmen – hunters
brach – female hound
sentinel'd – protected
sooth – truth
chidings – voices
scant – rare
booty – treasure (here meaning the prey being hunted)
hied – headed
gouts – splashes
besprent – sprinkled
suppliant – asking forgiveness
adieu – farewell
rue – regret
decked – decorated

ACTIVITIES

1 Narrative structure

The poem is easier to understand if you hear it read aloud – for example, by your teacher or a confident reader in your class. After you have heard it, focus on the story. If you were telling it in an adventure comic format for young children how would you relate it in twelve stages?

Put together a storyboard showing the images you would use. The real test is not whether you can draw, but whether you can reduce the storyline to just twelve frames. Quickly sketch each frame, then label what is happening. Compare your narrative with others in the class.

2 Verse form

The poem is written in quatrains (4-line verses) with an ABAB rhyme scheme. It has a steady rhythm. What effect does the poetic structure of the poem have on its meaning? Working on your own or in a pair, decide whether you agree, disagree, or neither agree nor disagree with these statements.

a The rhythm and rhyme make it fast-moving and dramatic.

b The structure holds our attention.

c The rhythm echoes the sound of horses' hooves.

d The rhyme scheme creates an old-fashioned feel to the poem.

e The story wouldn't be as entertaining in prose.

f The old-fashioned language adds to the atmosphere.

g The old-fashioned language gets in the way of the storyline.

h The poem contains too much description.

3 Language dating

As soon as you begin to read the poem, you can tell it was written a long time ago. But how? What are the main clues? Look through the poem for examples of archaic (old-fashioned) language such as:

a words we don't use any more

b words that are sometimes used in comedy programmes set in the past, but which are not part of modern standard English

c words that have been compressed or shortened for their effect

d places where the word order feels different from the way we might write today.

PRE-1900
Bishop Hatto
by Robert Southey

This narrative from the nineteenth century has many of the features of traditional story poems – a lively rhythm, a bloodthirsty storyline and an emphasis on plot rather than description or character.

Word Bank

repair – make their way, go

countenance – face

myriads – tens of thousands

beads – rosary beads, used for praying

tell – count

whetted – sharpened

Bishop Hatto

The summer and autumn had been so wet
That in winter the corn was growing yet;
'Twas a piteous sight to see all around
The grain lie rotting on the ground.   ①

5 Every day the starving poor
Crowded around Bishop Hatto's door,
For he had a plentiful last-year's store,
And all the neighbourhood could tell
His granaries were furnish'd well.   ②

10 At last Bishop Hatto appointed a day
To quiet the poor without delay;
He bade them to his great barn repair,
And they should have food for the winter there.   ③

Rejoiced such tidings good to hear,
15 The poor folk flock'd from far and near;
The great barn was full as it could hold
Of women and children, and young and old.   ④

Then when he saw it could hold no more,
Bishop Hatto he made fast the door,
20 And while for mercy on Christ they call,
He set fire to the barn and burnt them all.   ⑤

'I' faith, 'tis an excellent bonfire!' quoth he,
'And the country is greatly obliged to me,
For ridding it in these times forlorn
25 Of rats, that only consume the corn.'   ⑥

So then to his palace returned he,
And he sat down to supper merrily,
And he slept that night like an innocent man.
But Bishop Hatto never slept again.   ⑦

30 In the morning as he enter'd the hall,
Where his picture hung against the wall,
A sweat like death all over him came;
For the rats had eaten it out of the frame.   ⑧

As he look'd there came a man from his farm,
35 He had a countenance white with alarm;
'My lord, I open'd your granaries this morn,
And the rats had eaten all your corn.'   ⑨

93

Another came running presently,
And he was pale as pale could be;
40 'Fly! my Lord Bishop, fly!' quoth he,
'Ten thousand rats are coming this way –
The Lord forgive you for yesterday!'

⑩

Bishop Hatto fearfully hasten'd away,
And he crossed the Rhine without delay,
45 And reach'd his tower, and barr'd with care
All the windows, doors, and loopholes there.

⑪

He laid him down and closed his eyes,
But soon a scream made him arise;
He started, and saw two eyes of flame
50 On his pillows from whence the screaming came.

⑫

He listen'd and look'd; it was only the cat;
But the Bishop grew more fearful for that,
For she sat screaming, mad with fear,
At the army of rats that was drawing near.

⑬

55 For they have swum over the river so deep,
And they have climb'd the shores so steep,
And up the tower their way is bent,
To do the work for which they were sent.

⑭

They are not to be told by the dozen or score;
60 By thousands they come, and by myriads and more;
Such numbers had never been heard of before,
Such a judgement had never been witness'd of yore.

⑮

Down on his knees the Bishop fell,
And faster and faster his beads did he tell,
65 As louder and louder drawing near
The gnawing of their teeth he could hear.

⑯

And in at the windows, and in at the door,
And through the walls helter-skelter they pour,
And down from the ceiling, and up through the floor,
70 From the right and left, from behind and before,
From within and without, from above and below,
And all at once to the Bishop they go.

⑰

They have whetted their teeth against the stones,
And now they pick the Bishop's bones;
75 They gnaw'd the flesh from every limb,
For they were sent to do judgement on him!

⑱

ACTIVITIES

1 Tracing the storyline

What happens in the poem? Use a grid like the one below to reduce the poem to five or so main steps.

1

⬇

2

⬇

3

⬇

4

⬇

5

2 Narrative structure

Like many narratives, the poem tells its story using different tenses. Sometimes it uses the past tense as in line 18: 'Then when he saw it could hold no more'. Sometimes it uses the present tense as in line 74: 'And now they pick the Bishop's bones'.

Look at how the writer signals the tense here – partly through the verbs he uses (<u>saw</u> rather than <u>sees</u>; <u>pick</u> rather than <u>picked</u>); and partly through the adverbs he uses – <u>then</u> and <u>now</u>.

The poem is written in eighteen sections, each of which has been numbered.

a Write down the numbers 1–18, then against each number write down which tense the section uses – past, present, or a combination of the two?

b Look for the places where the writer switches from the past to the present tense. Why might he do this? Does it make the storyline more immediate, more dramatic, more terrifying, more relevant? What happens if you change the past tense verbs to the present tense and the present tense verbs to the past? Does the whole storyline begin to fall apart? Experiment and see what the effect is.

3 Opinions

The poem was written in the early nineteenth century and is often regarded as a poem for children.

a What clues can you find that the poem was not written recently?

b Do you think it's a suitable poem to read with children? If so, what ages do you think the children should be?

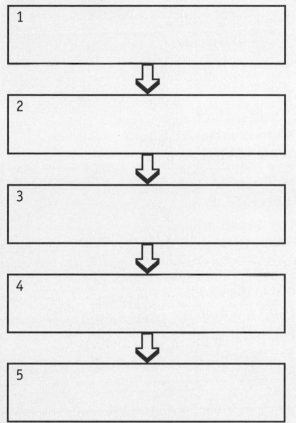

CLOSE READING

Fable

by Janos Pilinszky

A fable is an old story with a message. This one tells a modern tale. It comes from Hungary, and was translated into English by Ted Hughes.

Fable

Once upon a time
there was a lonely wolf
lonelier than the angels.

He happened to come to a village.
5 He fell in love with the first house he saw.

Already he loved its walls
the caresses of its bricklayers.
But the window stopped him.

In the room sat people.
10 Apart from God nobody ever
found them so beautiful
as this child-like beast.

So at night he went into the house.
He stopped in the middle of the room
15 and never moved from there any more.

He stood all through the night, with wide eyes
and on into the morning when he was beaten to death.

Questions

a Look again at the opening three lines. What kind of story do they lead the reader to expect?

b What impression do we get of the wolf? How does the writer encourage us to feel sympathy for him?

c The poem shocks us because of its brutal ending. Look also at the way the writer uses contrasting language: some parts of the poem use the kinds of word we expect in fairy-tales and legends. The end of the poem uses an unemotional phrase to describe the killing of the wolf. Write down an example of each kind of vocabulary.

d Like many narratives, this one feels as if it has a moral or message. What would you say the moral of the story is?

e Would this story work just as well in prose as in poetry or does the poetry give it a special power? Write a brief paragraph explaining your response.

Lyric poems

Starting Points

A lyric poem usually describes a single significant event in the poet's life.
The event may seem to be trivial or apparently unimportant, but the
poet usually reflects on its powerful influence. The poems in this unit
will help develop your familiarity with lyric poetry.

Death of a Naturalist *by Seamus Heaney*

Seamus Heaney's poem looks back to a childhood incident – a spring spent
collecting frogspawn and taking it into school. When he returns to the scene
later in the year we learn about how both it and he have changed.

Death of a Naturalist

All year the flax-dam festered in the heart
Of the townland; green and heavy headed
Flax had rotted there, weighted down by huge sods.
Daily it sweltered in the punishing sun.
5 Bubbles gargled delicately, bluebottles
Wove a strong gauze of sound around the smell.
There were dragon-flies, spotted butterflies,
But best of all was the warm thick slobber
Of frogspawn that grew like clotted water
10 In the shade of the banks. Here, every spring
I would fill jampotfuls of the jellied
Specks to range on window-sills at home,
On shelves at school, and wait and watch until
The fattening dots burst into nimble-
15 Swimming tadpoles. Miss Walls would tell us how
The daddy frog was called a bullfrog
And how he croaked and how the mammy frog
Laid hundreds of little eggs and this was
Frogspawn. You could tell the weather by frogs too
20 For they were yellow in the sun and brown
In rain.
          Then one hot day when fields were rank
With cowdung in the grass the angry frogs
Invaded the flax-dam; I ducked through hedges
25 To a coarse croaking that I had not heard
Before. The air was thick with a bass chorus.

Word Bank

naturalist – someone who studies nature

flax-dam – artificial pond in which flax is soaked to soften it. Flax is a plant used in the Irish linen-making industry

gauze – fine see-through material

rank – foul-smelling

obscene – disgusting

vengeance – revenge

Right down the dam gross-bellied frogs were cocked
On sods; their loose necks pulsed like sails. Some
                                                      hopped:

30 The slap and plop were obscene threats. Some sat
Poised like mud grenades, their blunt heads farting.
I sickened, turned, and ran. The great slime kings
Were gathered there for vengeance and I knew
That if I dipped my hand the spawn would clutch it.

ACTIVITIES

1 Senses

Seamus Heaney creates a powerful scene based on looking for tadpoles and finding they have turned into frogs. Look at how he uses the senses – sight, sound, smell, touch, taste – in the poem to create its atmosphere. Which ones does he use most? Find as many examples as you can.

2 Contrasts

In the first section of the poem, Seamus Heaney creates an idyllic (highly positive) scene. In contrast, the second section is like a nightmare. Look at these examples of positive and negative images, and comment on the picture they create in your mind. An example is done for you.

Positive	Negative
'... warm thick slobber / Of frogspawn' (lines 8–9) *Comment:* although we usually think of slobber as something unpleasant, here the child finds it fascinating. The fact that it is 'warm' shows that it is quite positive.	'... fields were rank / With cowdung ...' (lines 22–3)
'Bubbles gargled delicately' (line 5)	'The slap and plop were obscene threats.' (line 30)
'... wait and watch until / The fattening dots burst into nimble- / Swimming tadpoles' (lines 13–15)	'The great slime kings / Were gathered there for vengeance ...' (lines 32–3)

ACTIVITIES

3 Structure

Look more closely at the way Seamus Heaney structures his lyric poem. The two sections create a strong sense of contrast: the young child collecting frogspawn and then the older boy encountering the frogs.

Working on your own or in pairs, see if you can find some examples of the following techniques used to create contrast.

Section 1

a The poet uses vocabulary that makes the boy in the first section sound young, innocent and excited.

b He uses adverbs of place – <u>here</u> and <u>there</u> – to make the scene visual and immediate.

c He uses the rhythm of his sentences to imitate the speech style of a primary school teacher.

Section 2

a The poet uses an adverb of time to create an immediate contrast with the events of section one.

b He uses vocabulary that has echoes of vulgarity to show how the boy is in an older world.

c He uses some short sentences to create a contrast with the joyful, flowing style of section 1.

4 Comparison

Write two paragraphs about the poem, comparing sections 1 and 2. Focus your comments on the way the boy's response to nature changes in the poem.

● What does he find exciting in section 1? How does Seamus Heaney show the reader this excitement?

● How have the boy's feelings changed by section 2? How does Seamus Heaney emphasise this contrast?

Use short quotations from the poem to support your points.

In the first section the boy is attracted to the lively, exciting environment. The boy seems innocent, and perhaps a little gullible, for example when he says, 'You could tell the weather by frogs.' His voice here seems breathless and it sounds as though he is repeating something he has learnt from his teacher. Miss Walls was obviously a strong influence because he says, 'Miss Walls would tell us ...' and then he lists the different facts she has told the class. This all makes the child seem young and rather innocent.

The sentence makes it clear straight away which part of the poem we're looking at.

Quotation integrated into the sentence, rather than stuck separately on its own — this keeps it flowing.

Good that the answer looks at the effect of the language.

Another good use of a quotation followed by further comment on what it shows us.

For a Five-Year-Old *by Fleur Adcock*

Fleur Adcock's poem explores the way we 'cheat' when dealing with children. It's one rule for us and one rule for them. As you read the poem, look at its carefully devised structure – the rhyme scheme and the precisely chosen words. It shows how a lyric poem can capture a moment with the exactness of a photograph.

For a Five-Year-Old

A snail is climbing up the window-sill
Into your room, after a night of rain.
You call me in to see, and I explain
That it would be unkind to leave it there:
5 It might crawl to the floor; we must take care
That no one squashes it. You understand,
And carry it outside, with careful hand,
To eat a daffodil.

I see, then, that a kind of faith prevails:
10 Your gentleness is moulded still by words
From me, who have trapped mice and shot wild birds,
From me, who drowned your kittens, who betrayed
Your closest relatives, and who purveyed
The harshest kind of truth to many another.
15 But that is how things are: I am your mother,
And we are kind to snails.

Word Bank

prevails – survives
purveyed – carried

ACTIVITIES

1 Understanding

Like Seamus Heaney's 'Death of a Naturalist', this poem is in two halves. You probably found the first half quite straightforward. The more complex ideas are in Section 2. Use the statements below to help you understand the meaning of the poem. Of course, you're welcome to disagree with the views given here and come up with your own interpretation of the poem.

Section 1

a This describes an incident when a young child takes her mother's advice and carries a snail outdoors.

Section 2

a The mother feels that she's a hypocrite – she's often done and said things to hurt people, and yet here she's telling the child to be kind.

b The mother worries about the future for her child.

c The mother is reminded that the words she speaks to a child carry great weight.

d The mother sees how big an influence she is on the child.

e The mother feels that she is having to hide her own cruelty.

2 Structure

Below are some comments about the two sections of the poem. For each, one decide whether you agree or disagree, then try to find an example from the poem to support it.

Comment	Agree or disagree?	Example
Section 1 is a short narrative.		
Section 2 is a reflection.		
Section 1 is chiefly about the child.		
Section 2 is chiefly about the mother.		
Section 1 makes the world seem simple and straightforward.		
Section 2 makes the world seem complicated and sometimes unpleasant.		
The image of nature in section 1 is positive.		
The image of nature in section 2 is negative.		

3 Narrative voice

Section 1 uses the personal pronouns 'I', 'You' and 'We'. Section 2 chiefly uses 'I' and 'me'. What does this show about the way the poem develops in the second half?

Full Moon and Little Frieda *by Ted Hughes*

Ted Hughes is one of the most respected poets of our time. His early work was criticised by some people for its violence: he appeared at times to relish the aggression of the natural world. But his nature poetry is also full of wonder and excitement – as is this poem, a personal account of himself with his young daughter, Frieda. Like all small children she is excited by what she sees – in this case the moon. Ted Hughes can barely contain his excitement at seeing her sense of wonder.

Full Moon and Little Frieda

A cool small evening shrunk to a dog bark and the clank
                                                                    of a bucket –
And you listening.
A spider's web, tense for the dew's touch.
5   A pail lifted, still and brimming – mirror
To tempt a first star to a tremor.

Cows are going home in the lane there, looping the hedges
                                        with their warm wreaths of breath –
A dark river of blood, many boulders,
10   Balancing unspilled milk.

'Moon!' you cry suddenly, 'Moon! Moon!'

The moon has stepped back like an artist gazing amazed
                                                                    at a work
That points at him amazed.

ACTIVITIES

1 Images

The poem is full of unusual images. Write them out and annotate the images, saying what you notice about them – like this:

A cool small evening shrunk to a dog bark and the clank of a bucket –

> **cool** suggests that it may be late – the heat of the day gone
>
> **small** – an unusual word to describe an evening; suggests that it's a special time, perhaps, shared with his daughter
>
> **shrunk** – perhaps because this is the only part of the evening he now remembers
>
> **dog bark** – use of senses (hearing) to capture the atmosphere
>
> **clank of bucket** – another sound; bucket used for milking the cows perhaps

See what ideas spring into your mind as you study these words more closely.

A pail lifted, still and brimming – mirror
To tempt a first star to a tremor. (lines 4–5)

A dark river of blood, many boulders,
Balancing unspilled milk. (lines 9–10)

The moon has stepped back like an artist
    gazing amazed
    at a work
That points at him amazed. (lines 13–14)

2 Audience

The poem is unusual because it uses the second person mode. This means rather than saying 'I' or 'she/he/they', it uses 'you'. The poem is addressed to 'you' – Frieda.

a What effect does this have? Does it make the reader feel less involved in the poem because it feels like a personal dialogue between the writer and his daughter? Or do we find it more interesting because of the unusual narrative voice?

b To test the effect, try replacing 'you' with 'she', and 'your' with 'her'. This will make it a third-person narrative. How does the effect change?

3 Lyric form

The text is a perfect example of a lyric poem, taking one event and reflecting upon it. Now take the first line. How would it be written if it were the opening of a story or a sentence from an autobiography? Try writing the sentence in prose (everyday language) so that it communicates the same ideas, but in a style we might expect from prose rather than poetry.

You could then try to write the next few lines of the poem in prose, noting the decisions you make.

Write a few sentences about the changes you had to make and how well your version works.

PRE-1900
Elegy *by Chidiock Tichborne*

This is a difficult poem on a first reading –
but don't be put off. The activities will
show you how to get to grips with the
meaning and the language.

Chidiock Tichborne was executed
for treason in 1586 at the age of
28. He wrote this brief elegy, or
lament for his life, in the Tower
of London, knowing that he
would soon be dead.

Elegy

My prime of youth is but a frost of cares,
  My feast of joy is but a dish of pain,
My crop of corn is but a field of tares,
  And all my good is but vain hope of gain;
5   The day is past, and yet I saw no sun,
  And now I live, and now my life is done.

My tale was heard and yet it is not told,
  My fruit is fallen and yet my leaves are green,
My youth is spent and yet I am not old,
10   I saw the world and yet I am not seen;
  My thread is cut and yet it is not spun,
  And now I live, and now my life is done.

I sought my death and found it in the womb,
  I looked for life and saw it was a shade,
15 I trod the earth and knew it was my tomb,
  And now I die, and now I am but made;
My glass is full, and yet my glass is run,
  And now I live, and now my life is done.

Word Bank

tares – weeds

sought – looked for

glass – an hour-glass
which, like an egg-timer,
measures time in sand

ACTIVITIES

1 Images

At the core of this poem is a single idea – 'I am about to die and yet I am not ready' – which the writer expresses through a variety of different images.

Take the second part of the idea first: 'I am not ready'. Look at some of the images that express this idea. Try to say something about each image – what picture you get, what it reminds you of, words you like/dislike/don't know and so on – like this:

> **Paradox**
> a statement which contains opposite ideas: 'I am old but I am young'. On the surface, paradoxes are contradictions. They allow the writer to show confusion, frustration or tension.

Images expressing the idea of 'I am not ready'	Your comments
My crop of corn	Corn gives an image of something natural that is still growing in nature.
I saw no sun	Suggests he hasn't yet had the full experience of life — there are still things to do and see.
[my tale] is not told	
my leaves are green	
[my thread] is not spun	

Find two more examples of images expressing this idea of wasted youth.

Now take the first part of the idea – 'I am about to die'. One example is given for you. This time find four examples and comment on each one, as above.

Images expressing the idea of 'I am about to die'~	Your comments
My fruit is fallen	Suggests he is dying before he is ready.

Which of the images do you think works best? Which is hardest to understand?

2 Structure

The poem is built around a series of paradoxes – which simply means opposite ideas placed side by side ('And now I live, and now my life is done'). At first glance, the sections of the poem look similar – but they're not. This gives us some clues about the way the writer's thoughts develop. If we just highlight the words used to link the ideas, in the first verse, looks like this:

idea ... **but** ... paradox
idea ... **but** ... paradox
idea ... **but** ... paradox
idea ... **but** ... paradox
idea ... **and yet** ... paradox
And now ... idea .... **and now** ... paradox

By taking this basic structure you can see how the poem works. The last line of each verse breaks the pattern. Try to describe the effect this has – what impression it creates.

CLOSE READING

The Smell of Chrysanthemums
by Elizabeth Jennings

Elizabeth Jennings writes about something we all sometimes experience – the way a sound or smell can suddenly prompt unexpected emotions. Here the smell of chrysanthemums launches a host of feelings and memories.

The Smell of Chrysanthemums

The chestnut leaves are toasted. Conkers spill
Upon the pavements. Gold is vying with
Yellow, ochre, brown. There is a feel
Of dyings and departures. Smoky breath
5   Rises and I know how Winter comes
      When I can smell the rich chrysanthemums.

It is so poignant and it makes me mourn
For what? The going year? The sun's eclipse?
All these and more. I see the dead leaves burn
10 And everywhere the Summer lies in heaps.
     I close my eyes and feel how Winter comes
     With acrid incense of chrysanthemums.

I shall not go to school again and yet
There's an old sadness that disturbs me most.
15 The nights come early; every bold sunset
Tells me that Autumn soon will be a ghost,
     But I know best how Winter always comes
     In the wide scent of strong chrysanthemums.

Word Bank

chrysanthemums – brightly coloured flowers

ochre – brownish yellow

poignant – sad

acrid – bitter

incense – perfume

CLOSE READING

Advice on reading

This section develops your ability to respond to the language of a single poem. Start by reading the poem through once, perhaps jotting down notes about your first impressions. Then look at the questions below. What areas are you being asked to focus on? Now read the poem carefully once more, again making notes of ideas that occur to you. Remember that responding to an unseen poem will often require you to read it through carefully three or more times.

Advice on writing

Remember to answer each question in a full sentence or paragraph. Support your ideas with examples from the text wherever possible. Try to quote just a few words at a time rather than copying out chunks of the text.

Questions

a The poem is written in three verses. Say, in a sentence or two, what each one seems to be about.

b How does Elizabeth Jennings create a powerful sense of autumn?

c Explain what you think she means in lines 13–14 by: 'I shall not go to school again and yet / There's an old sadness that disturbs me most.'

d The last two lines of each stanza talk about winter. What are the writer's feelings about this season?

e In what ways do you think this poem is a typical lyric poem?

Comparisons

Introduction

One of the skills that you will need to develop for GCSE English is comparing poems. Whichever examination syllabus your school follows, there is a requirement that students should be able to compare texts. Some exam papers place two texts side by side and ask you to write about the similarities and differences. You might be asked to compare two poems, or a poem and an autobiography, or a combination of other kinds of texts.

The final unit of this book therefore aims to teach you some of the skills you'll need for your English work in the future.

COMPARISON 1: *Two poems*

Being-in-love *by Roger McGough*

'Stop all the clocks, cut off the telephone' *by W. H. Auden*

These two poems explore feelings of love. The first is 'unrequited love' – love for someone that isn't returned: a lonely kind of feeling. The second is a deep love for someone who has recently died.

Being-in-love

you are so very beautiful
i cannot help admiring
your eyes so often sadnessful
and lips so kissinspiring

5 i think about my being-in-love
and touch the flesh you wear so well
i think about my being-in-love
and wish you were as well
                              as well
10 and wish you were as well

Roger McGough

108

'Stop all the clocks, cut off the telephone'

Stop all the clocks, cut off the telephone,
Prevent the dog from barking with a juicy bone,
Silence the pianos and with muffled drum
Bring out the coffin, let the mourners come.

5   Let aeroplanes circle moaning overhead
Scribbling on the sky the message He Is Dead,
Put crêpe bows round the white necks of the public doves,
Let the traffic policemen wear black cotton gloves.

He was my North, my South, my East and West,
10 My working week and my Sunday rest,
My noon, my midnight, my talk, my song;
I thought that love would last for ever: I was wrong.

The stars are not wanted now: put out every one;
Pack up the moon and dismantle the sun;
15 Pour away the ocean and sweep up the wood;
For nothing now can ever come to any good.

W. H. Auden

Word Bank

black cotton gloves – in times of national mourning, policemen would wear these

dismantle – take apart

ACTIVITIES

Being-in-love

1 Narrative voice

What impression do you get of the narrator? Is the person male or female? Around what age? Is this the first time s/he's been in love? What might the lack of capital letters tell you about the narrator?

2 Vocabulary

Why do you think the poet uses two made-up words: 'sadnessful' (line 3) and 'kissinspiring' (line 4)? Do they communicate meanings that real words wouldn't, or does he perhaps use them to show us something about the narrator?

3 Rhyme scheme

The poem has an ABAB structure – though it is varied a little in the second verse. The first verse has slightly odd rhymes because of the made-up words. The second verse uses very heavy rhymes because the same words are used so often.

Why might the poet be using rhyme in this way? Is there anything he might be telling us about the character of the narrator?

4 Personal response

What do you like or dislike about this poem?

What do you like or dislike about its style?

Stop all the clocks ...

1 Images

It is clear from this poem that the narrator is deeply upset. How does the writer use images to show the strength of his grief? You might comment on the specific examples below and what they show about the narrator's feelings.

a 'Stop all the clocks' (line 1)

b 'Let aeroplanes circle moaning overhead' (line 5)

c 'The stars are not wanted now: put out every one' (line 13)

2 Rhythm

The poem has four verses. Read each one again. Is the rhythm the same in each? Use the prompts below to sharpen your response to the rhythm of the poem. See whether you agree or disagree with the comments.

a One verse has a faster rhythm than the others – it has a definite beat, moving us quickly.

b Another verse feels unpoetic – instead it feels like everyday conversation.

c The rhythm throughout the poem is jumpy and disjointed. It rarely flows. This is a sign of the state of the narrator's emotions – a smooth, regular rhythm would seem out of place.

3 Personal response

Some readers find the poem deeply moving. For others it has little effect. What do you think? Talk or write about features of the poem you especially like or dislike. You might comment on:

- the content – what is being described
- the structure
- the use of rhythm and rhyme
- other forms of sound patterning
- the images.

A MAKING COMPARISONS

Use the prompts that follow to discuss the similarities and differences between the two poems.

a Which poem expresses a stronger sense of love? How can you tell?

b Which is more lighthearted? How can you tell?

c Which text feels more like a poem? In what way?

d Which text tells you more about the narrator? Can you give examples?

e Which text is more formal?

f Which text has the more unusual use of language?

g How do the texts use imagery differently? What kinds of image do you notice?

h How do the poems use sound patterning – rhythm, rhyme, onomatopoeia, alliteration? (Remember to use the Glossary to check the meaning of these terms.) What do they add to the meaning?

i What do you like about each poem? What do you dislike?

j Which poem do you prefer overall? Why?

B WRITING ABOUT THE TEXTS

Your commentary should give a personal response supported by brief quotations from the texts. Remember to say what you notice and what you think.

● Write a paragraph describing what each poem is about – its content and ideas.

● Write a paragraph noting the similarities and differences between the vocabulary of the poems – the kinds of word each writer uses (are they formal, colloquial [chatty], emotive, modern, archaic?).

● Write about the structure of the two poems – how the ideas are organised.

● Write about other features you notice – use of sound patterning, images, interesting language features.

● Conclude by writing about which poem you prefer, and why.

COMPARISON 2: *Prose/Poetry*

Rabbit in mixer survives *by Roger McGough*

Roger McGough takes a newspaper article from the *Daily Telegraph,* then uses a poem to give a different view of the story. What differences do you notice between the two texts?

Rabbit in mixer survives

A BABY RABBIT FELL into a quarry's mixing machine yesterday and came out in the middle of a concrete block. But the rabbit still had the strength to dig its way free before the block set.

The tiny creature was scooped up with 30 tons of sand, then swirled and pounded through the complete mixing process. Mr Michael Hooper, the machine operator, found the rabbit shivering on top of the solid concrete block, its coat stiff with fragments. A hole from the middle of the block and paw marks showed the escape route.

Mr Reginald Denslow, manager of J R Pratt and Sons' quarry at Kilmington, near Axminster, Devon, said: 'This rabbit must have a lot more than nine lives to go through this machine. I just don't know how it avoided being suffocated, ground, squashed or cut in half.' With the 30 tons of sand, it was dropped into a weighing hopper and carried by conveyor to an overhead mixer where it was whirled around with gallons of water.

From there the rabbit was swept to a machine which hammers wet concrete into blocks by pressure of 100 lb per square inch. The rabbit was encased in a block eighteen inches long, nine inches high and six inches thick. Finally the blocks were ejected on to the floor to dry and the dazed rabbit clawed itself free. 'We cleaned him up, dried him by the electric fire, then he hopped away,' Mr Denslow said.

Article published in *The Daily Telegraph*

Rabbit in mixer survives

'Tell us a story Grandad'
The bunny rabbits implored
'About the block of concrete
Out of which you clawed.'

5 'Tell every gory detail
Of how you struggled free
From the teeth of the Iron Monster
And swam through a quicksand sea.'

'How you battled with the Humans
10 (And the part we like the most)
Your escape from the raging fire
When they held you there to roast.'

The old adventurer smiled
And waved a wrinkled paw
15 'All right children, settle down,
I'll tell it just once more.'

His thin nose started twitching
Near-blind eyes began to flood
As the part that doesn't age
20 Drifted back to bunnyhood.

When spring was king of the seasons
And days were built to last
When thunder was merely thunder
Not a distant quarry blast.

25 How, leaving the warren one morning
Looking for somewhere to play,
He'd wandered far into the woods
And there had lost his way.

When suddenly without warning
30 The earth gave way, and he fell
Off the very edge of the world
Into the darkness of Hell.

Sharp as the colour of a carrot
On a new-born bunny's tongue
35 Was the picture he recalled
Of that day when he was young.

Trance-formed now by the memory
His voice was close to tears
But the story he was telling
40 Was falling on deaf ears.

There was giggling and nudging
And lots of 'sssh – he'll hear'
For it was a trick, a game they played
Grown crueller with each year.

45 'Poor old Grandad' they tittered
As they one by one withdrew
'He's told it all so often
He now believes it's true.'

Young rabbits need fresh carrots
50 And his had long grown stale
So they left the old campaigner
Imprisoned in his tale.

Petrified by memories
Haunting ever strong
55 Encased in a block of time
Eighteen inches long.

* * *

Alone in a field in Devon
An old rabbit is sitting, talking,
When out of the wood, at the edge
of the world,
60 A man with a gun comes walking.

Roger McGough

ACTIVITIES

Rabbit in mixer survives
(Newspaper article)

1 Understanding

a How did the rabbit get caught in the concrete mixer in the first place?

b How do phrases like 'the tiny creature' make us feel sympathy for the rabbit?

c How does the writer show the personality of the rabbit?

2 Language features

How would you know, even if you hadn't been told, that this text came from a newspaper? Look for clues in:

- the layout of the text
- the first sentence, which summarises the whole story
- the way the writer describes people ('Mr Michael Hooper ...')
- the way the writer quotes the words people have spoken
- the way the writer tells the story.

'Rabbit in mixer survives'
(Poem)

1 Understanding

a Why do the young rabbits want to hear Grandad's story?

b How would you describe their attitude to Grandad – respectful, in awe, poking fun at him or neutral? Why?

c How can you tell that Grandad finds the memory emotional?

d How does the writer encourage us to feel sympathy for Grandad?

2 Structure

a Who is speaking in the first three verses of the poem?

b Who speaks during the rest of the poem?

c Look at the last verse. It is separated from the rest of the poem by three asterisks. What is happening here? In what ways is this last section different?

3 Verse form

The poem is written (mostly) in quatrains (4-line verses) with an ABCB structure and a strong sense of rhythm. How does this help us to get involved in the storyline?

A MAKING COMPARISONS

Use the prompts below to discuss the similarities and differences between the two texts.

a Which text is easier to follow? Why?

b Which text makes the rabbit victim more sympathetic? How?

c Which text contains more detail of the moments in the mixer?

d Which text makes you want to keep reading more? Why?

e Why do you think Roger McGough presents the event as something that happened in the past – rather than showing it in the present?

f What techniques does Roger McGough use to help us see the thoughts and feelings of the rabbit?

g Do you think his poem is faithful to what actually happened – or has it become an almost fictional version?

h What do you like or dislike about each text?

B WRITING ABOUT THE TEXTS

Your commentary should give a personal response supported by brief quotations from the texts. Remember to say what you notice and what you think.

- Write about the way the first text tells the story – the features that are typical of newspaper journalism.

- Now compare the way the poem tells the story – including the use of characterisation, rhythm and rhyme to hook our interest.

- Describe any differences in detail between the two texts – for example, the presentation of the rabbit.

- Write about the way the two texts enhance each other – one giving us some information; the other helping us to imagine how the rabbit might have felt.

- Conclude by describing what you enjoyed or disliked in these two texts.

COMPARISON 3: *Factual Writing/Fiction/Poetry*

A Night to Remember *by Walter Lord*

Every Man for Himself *by Beryl Bainbridge*

'The Convergence of the Twain' *by Thomas Hardy*

This section contains a three-way comparison. The texts tell the story of one of the twentieth century's most terrible human disasters – the sinking of the *Titanic* in 1912. Walter Lord's book is a classic factual account of the events of the evening. Beryl Bainbridge's award-winning novel re-presents the moment of the collision with the iceberg. Thomas Hardy's poem reflects on the significance of the collision and what it shows about human civilisation.

A Night to Remember

Frederick Fleet was one of six lookouts carried by the *Titanic*, and the lookouts didn't worry about passenger problems. They were the 'eyes of the ship', and on this particular night Fleet had been warned to watch especially for icebergs.

So far, so good. On duty at 10 o'clock . . . a few words about the ice problem with lookout Reginald Lee, who shared the same watch . . . a few more words about the cold . . . but mostly just silence, as the two men stared into the darkness.

Now the watch was almost over, and still there was nothing unusual. Just the night, the stars, the biting cold, the wind that whistled through the rigging as the *Titanic* raced across the calm, black sea at 22.5 knots. It was almost 11.40 p.m. on Sunday, 14 April 1912.

Suddenly Fleet saw something directly ahead, even darker than the darkness. At first it was small (about the size, he thought, of two tables put together) but every second it grew larger and closer. Quickly Fleet banged the crow's-nest bell three times, the warning of danger ahead. At the same time he lifted the phone and rang the bridge.

'What did you see?' asked a calm voice at the other end.

'Iceberg right ahead,' replied Fleet.

'Thank you,' acknowledged the voice with curiously detached courtesy. Nothing more was said.

For the next thirty-seven seconds Fleet and Lee stood quietly side by side, watching the ice draw nearer. Now they were almost on top of it, and still the ship didn't turn. The berg towered wet and glistening far above the fore-castle deck, and both men braced themselves for a crash. Then, miraculously, the bow began to swing to port. At the last second the stem shot into the clear, and the ice glided swiftly by along the starboard side. It looked to Fleet like a close shave.

At this moment Quartermaster George Thomas Rowe was standing watch on the after bridge. For him too, it had been an uneventful night – just the sea, the stars, the biting cold. As he paced the deck, he noticed what he and his mates called 'whiskers 'round the light' – tiny splinters of ice in the air, fine as dust, that gave off myriads of bright colours whenever caught in the glow of the deck lights.

Then suddenly he felt a curious motion break the steady rhythm of the engines. It was a little like coming alongside a dock wall rather heavily. He glanced forward – and stared again. A windjammer, sails set, seemed to be passing along the starboard side. Then he realized it was an iceberg, towering perhaps 100 feet above the water. The next instant it was gone, drifting astern into the dark.

Meanwhile, down below in the first-class dining-saloon on D deck, four other members of the *Titanic*'s crew were sitting round one of the tables. The last diner had long since departed, and now the big white Jacobean room was empty except for this single group. They were dining-saloon stewards, indulging in the time-honoured pastime of all stewards off duty – they were gossiping about their passengers.

Then, as they sat there talking, a faint grinding jar seemed to come from somewhere deep inside the ship. It was not much, but enough to break the conversation and rattle the silver that was set for breakfast next morning.

Walter Lord

Every Man for Himself

Butt and he left at half-past eleven. I know that because Butt took out his watch and expressed surprise at the lateness of the hour. I guess he was desperate to get to his bed. They had been gone no more than ten minutes – Ginsberg had ordered a whisky and Charlie and I had just won three tricks in succession – when suddenly the room juddered; the lights flickered and Ginsberg's cigarette case, which sat at his elbow, jolted to the floor. It was the sound accompanying the juddering that startled us, a long drawn-out tearing, like a vast length of calico slowly ripping apart. Melchett said, 'We're in collision with another ship,' and with that we threw down our cards, ran to the doors, sprinted through the Palm Court and out on to the deck. A voice called, 'We've bumped an iceberg – there it goes,' but though I peered into the darkness I could see nothing. From somewhere forward we heard laughter, voices excitedly shouting. Coming to the starboard rail I looked down on to the well of the third class recreation area; there were chunks of ice spilling and sliding in every direction, all shapes and sizes, glittering under the light of the foremast. Steerage passengers, most in their ragged nightclothes, were chucking it at each other as though playing snowballs. Hopper raced off to go down there and join in the fun. Charlie and I found it too cold to linger and hurried back indoors. A dozen or so men had poured out of the smoke-room and were milling about in the foyer, pestering the stewards for information. Astor was there, still dressed but without his tie, leaning down to shout into the ear of Seefax who had been woken from sleep in the library and now sat on the staircase with his stick raised like a weapon. Everyone had a different explanation for whatever it was that had jarred the ship; Ginsberg swore we had lost a propeller, but what did he know?

We couldn't resume our game until Hopper returned, which he did quite soon, triumphantly carrying a lump of ice in his handkerchief. He thrust it under my nose and it smelt rank, a bit like a sliver of rotten mackerel. He dropped it into Ginsberg's whisky when the poor devil wasn't looking.

We must have played for another ten minutes, by which time Hopper said he'd had enough. Remembering Andrews' injunction that I should read while others slept, I decided to spend an hour in the library. I was crossing the foyer when the man himself swept past on his way to the stairs. I didn't think he'd seen me but he said quite distinctly, 'Follow me. You may be needed.'

He led me up to the navigating bridge. Captain Smith was evidently expecting him because as we approached the wheelhouse the quartermaster flung open the door. I would have followed on Andrews' heels but he shouted over his shoulders that I was to wait outside. Through the glass panels I could see Smith and his first and second officers clustering about him. Ismay was there too, dressed in a fur coat and wearing carpet slippers. He seemed to be excluded, roaming up and down, hands in pockets.

I was glad I wasn't outdoors, for even in the comparative warmth of the bridge house I found myself shivering. The silence wrapped me like a cloak and it was only then that I realised the ship no longer moved. When I pressed my face to the window to look down at the sea there was nothing but darkness; when I tilted my head the blackness was fiery with stars.

Beryl Bainbridge

The Convergence of the Twain
(Lines on the loss of the *Titanic*)

I
IN a solitude of the sea
Deep from human vanity,
And the Pride of Life that planned her, stilly couches she.

II
Steel chambers, late the pyres
Of her salamandrine fires,
Cold currents thrid, and turn to rhythmic tidal lyres.

III
Over the mirrors meant
To glass the opulent
The sea-worm crawls – grotesque, slimed, dumb, indifferent.

IV
Jewels in joy designed
To ravish the sensuous mind
Lie lightless, all their sparkles bleared and black and blind.

V
Dim moon-eyed fishes near
Gaze at the gilded gear
And query : 'What does this vaingloriousness down here?' . . .

VI
Well: while was fashioning
This creature of cleaving wing.
The Immanent Will that stirs and urges everything

VII
Prepared a sinister mate
For her — so gaily great —
A Shape of Ice, for the time far and dissociate.

VIII
And as the smart ship grew
In stature, grace, and hue,
In shadowy silent distance grew the Iceberg too.

IX
Alien they seemed to be :
No mortal eye could see
The intimate welding of their later history,

X
Or sign that they were bent
By paths coincident
On being anon twin halves of one august event,

XI
Till the Spinner of the Years
Said 'Now!' And each one hears,
And consummation comes, and jars two hemispheres.

Thomas Hardy

5
10
15
20
25
30

Word Bank

vanity – pride

salamandrine – red-hot

thrid – thread

glass – reflect

opulent – wealthy

grotesque – ugly

indifferent – unfeeling

ravish the sensuous mind – impress the senses

vaingloriousness – empty boasting

Immanent Will – God

dissociate – separated

hue – colour

august – awe-inspiring

consummation – completion

ACTIVITIES

A Night to Remember
(Factual writing)

1 Genre study

How can you tell that this is a factual account rather than, say, a poem or an extract from a novel? Make some notes on the language features that help you to know this. Here are some suggestions.

- Look out for use of precise details – names, times, specific people in specific places.

- Notice the use of dialogue to show what people said – but think about this a little more. How could a writer know what words were actually spoken between people on a sinking ship? Do you think this conversation *has* be made up?

- Look at the way the story is told – step by step, as in a formal report. But look also for ways in which the writer builds suspense before the collision actually happens.

- Look at the vocabulary – is it specific and neutral and used to describe what happens rather than to have an emotional effect upon us?

Every Man for Himself
(Fiction)

1 Genre study

If you hadn't been told, would you know that this extract came from a fictional account, rather than an autobiography or poem? What features do you notice that help you to know it is from a novel?

Use the prompts below in your discussion.

- Look at the way the writer makes us view events through the eyes of a character. Why would you be unlikely to find this style in a formal report of the event? What effect does it have on us as we read the storyline? Do we get more or less involved because of the technique?

- Look at the language. Does it seem more descriptive than you'd expect in a factual text? Can you find examples? Is the writer's use of language designed to have an emotional effect upon us?

- How does the writer tell the story – can you see ways in which she creates suspense, keeping us guessing or making us wait for the next stage in the story?

- Does the fictional account allow the writer to show us scenes that a writer using real evidence could never use?

'The Convergence of the Twain' *(Poetry)*

1 Understanding

a How does the poet show the way the ship has been transformed?

b How can you tell that he seems critical of the *Titanic*?

c What hint is there that the collision was not an accident but an act of fate?

d How does the final line of the poem hint at the huge effect the loss of the *Titanic* had?

2 Genre study

a The poem has an unusual structure – 3-line verses with the same rhyme.

b Can you detect any strong rhythm or does the poem feel more like a speech or conversation?

c Does the rhyme make the event seem more or less serious?

d Is the vocabulary pompous and difficult in order to distance us from the actual event and make us think instead about what it shows about human beings?

e What types of sound patterning does the writer use (alliteration, onomatopoeia, repetition of words and sounds)? What do these add to the overall meaning?

A MAKING COMPARISONS

Use the prompts below to discuss the similarities and differences between the three texts.

a Which text gives the strongest impression of the actual collision?

b Which shows its human impact the most?

c Which text seems most critical of the whole *Titanic* enterprise?

d In which text is the author's attitude most obvious?

e Which text do you feel most involved in? Why?

f Which text is the most emotional?

g Which do you like most and least? Why?

B WRITING ABOUT THE TEXTS

Your commentary should give a personal response supported by brief quotations from the texts. Remember to write down what you notice and what you think.

a Start by writing about what each text shows of the collision itself. How much detail do they give? How involved do we feel?

b Talk about the writers' techniques to gain, and then hold, our attention – what makes us want to read on?

c Look more closely at the vocabulary each writer uses. How does each writer's choice of words differ?

d Look at the ways in which the writers structure their accounts of the event. What similarities and differences do you notice?

e Finally, write about which text you find most interesting and why.

Poetry writing assignments

These assignments have been created to help you to develop your poetry response through other forms of writing. Your teacher may want to advise you about which assignment is most appropriate for the poems you are studying.

Personal response

1   Write an imaginary letter to the author of a poem you have particularly enjoyed. Describe what you like about the poem. You might comment upon:

- its ideas
- the vocabulary
- its message
- use of rhythm and rhyme
- the structure
- its imagery.

If you wish, use the glossary which begins on page 124 to remind yourself of the meaning of these terms. When you write about the poem, try to support your points with specific references to the text.

2   Based upon poems you have enjoyed in this book, or on your own wider reading, put together a collection of three poems you particularly like. Then write an introduction to the poems aimed at someone who has not yet read them. Tell your reader:

- why you chose these poems
- what to look out for in the language
- briefly what they are about
- any unusual features you noticed.

Narrative voice

3   Choose a poem like 'The Listeners' (page 60) or 'The Haunted Lift' (page 50). Look again at the narrative voice in the poem – at who speaks to us. Now experiment with telling the storyline of the poem using a different narrator. For example, you might re-tell the tale of 'The Listeners' through the eyes of a phantom listener inside the house. Re-tell your chosen poem as a piece of narrative writing if you prefer, or have a go at writing it in verse.

4   Look again at some poems where the narrator speaks as 'I'. Choose one or two of the narrators and interview them about the experience they describe in the poem. You might, for example, interview Grandad Rabbit about his experience of being trapped in the concrete mixer (see page 113), as a way of imagining more details about the way it has affected him.

Continuations

5 Choose a poem you have enjoyed and write a continuation – another verse or section. Try to write as closely as possible in the style of the original poem. Then write a paragraph describing how successful you think you have been.

Other forms

6 Use a poem you find interesting as the basis for a newspaper article or diary entry. Imagine, for example, how 'The Haunted Lift' (page 50) might be re-presented as a newspaper story in a local paper.

Analysis

7 Choose a poem you find especially interesting and write it out. Then annotate it in detail. That means using arrows and underlinings to ask really detailed questions about the text, make comments about the words, and make observations about the structure and effect. Your final page should look like a mass of ideas surrounding the original poem.

8 Choose one poem and write a detailed line-by-line description of your response to it. In each line you might comment upon:

- the ideas and the way they are structured
- the vocabulary
- the way the lines are organised
- special effects – such as alliteration, imagery, personification
- use of rhythm and rhyme.

Describe what you notice in as much detail as you can. Conclude by writing about what you like or dislike about the poem.

Glossary of poetic terms

Adjectives

Adjectives are words which add extra information and meaning to nouns – <u>misty</u> mountains, <u>pale</u> faces, <u>deep</u> dungeons, <u>low</u> wages.

Adverbs

Adverbs tell us more about the verb. They show when, how or where something happens, like this:

verb	adverb
run	quickly
eat	noisily

These are easy adverbs to spot because they end in 'ly'. But there are other, less recognisable adverbs which tell us about time, manner and place – such as <u>often</u>, <u>now</u>, <u>yesterday</u>, <u>then</u>; <u>quite</u>, <u>even</u>, <u>nevertheless</u>; <u>there</u>, <u>here</u>.

Alliteration

Alliteration is a series of words that begin with the same sound. They help writers to create patterns in their language. Sometimes the words may be next to each other: '<u>a</u>bove <u>a</u>nd <u>a</u>round'; sometimes they may be further apart: 'The white clouds are <u>sc</u>udding across the blue <u>sk</u>y'.

Associations

Associations are the feelings certain words create in us. 'Black' is associated with death and evil. 'Light' is associated with clarity and truth. Associative words trigger our deeper thoughts and emotions. They are therefore useful to poets because they can call up a powerful emotional response.

Couplets and quatrains

These are two words to describe types of verse used in poetry. Just as in prose you would structure ideas in paragraphs, poets often use verses (or stanzas). Couplets are pairs of lines – as in the first section of 'Night Mail' (see page 64). If the two lines rhyme, we call them rhyming couplets. Quatrains are sets of four lines. They don't have to rhyme, but they usually do – line 2 and 4 rhyming and, sometimes, lines 1 and 3.

Imagery

Imagery is the word we use for a series of images. An image is a picture we see in our minds. Writers create images using the following main techniques.

a Simile: one thing is compared to another using the linking word <u>as</u> or <u>like</u> – for example, fast as lightning; leapt like a fox.

b Metaphor: one thing is compared to another but without use of the linking word <u>as</u> or <u>like</u> – for example, He was a tiger in battle; Rain is when the earth is television.

c Personification: an abstract concept (like time, death, hope) is presented as if it was a person or animal – for example, Death stalked the battlefields; Winter had claimed the world again.

Internal rhyme

We usually expect rhymes at the ends of the lines of poems. But sometimes poets use words in the middle of a line that rhyme with the word at the end. This increases the sense of sound patterns in the text.

Lyric poem

This is a poem that centres on a significant moment in the poet's life. It is usually about the emotions that the event creates – seeing a host of daffodils and thinking about their beauty; picking up a sleeping child, and reflecting on the love you feel.

Metaphor

A metaphor works like a simile. Remember that a simile compares two things using the words <u>as</u> or <u>like</u>. A metaphor also creates a comparison, without using those words. The simile 'dropped like a wet blanket' would be a metaphor if it said 'he was a wet blanket'. Metaphors are more compressed and direct than similes.

Narrative poem

A poem that tells a story. Early narrative poems, usually focused on one or two main characters, were called ballads.

Narrator

As in a novel, the narrator is the person who tells you a story. In 'You Being Born' (page 14), we are told of the birth by the narrator – the person who is 'I'.

Onomatopoeia

These are words that sound like the sounds they describe – crash, crack, buzz, murmur. We use them because they can make descriptions seem more vivid.

Paradox

A statement which contains opposite ideas: "I am old but I am young". On the surface, paradoxes are contradictions. They allow the writer to show confusion, frustration or tension.

Prose

Prose is the writing we see most – in newspapers, magazines, novels and leaflets. Prose is organised in sentences and paragraphs, whereas poetry is in lines and (usually) verses or stanzas. The language of poetry is usually more patterned.

Rhyme

Patterns of sound. Words can have full rhyme – like 'slime' and 'chime'; or half-rhyme, like 'heat' and 'heal'. We usually expect rhymes to occur at the end of lines, but poets also use internal rhyme – rhymes which take place within lines – like this: 'the cat and the bat went off for a walk ...'

Rhyme scheme

A rhyme scheme is the term we use to describe the way a writer organises rhyming words. In 'The Lion and Albert' (page 42) there are four lines to a verse. The second and fourth verses rhyme (fun ... son). If you were to write out the rhyme scheme, you usually use letters to show which lines rhyme with which. Each letter stands for a different line. So the rhyme scheme for this poem would be:

A Blackpool
B fun
C Ramsbottom
B son

Rhyming couplets

A style of poetry where one line rhymes with the line that comes straight after it. See the poem 'Prince Kano' (page 52) as an example.

Rhythm

We sometimes call this metre. It is the pattern of sounds created by a poet's choice and arrangement of words. Rhythm is based on the mixture of some syllables that are emphasised and some that are unstressed. Some sound patterns are regular, and create a strong effect on us: we can feel the rhythm inside us. Others use a less regular rhythm. Rhythm in language works as in music: different beats are put together in a certain pattern.

Stanza

When a poem is organised into groups of lines, with each group forming a distinct unit, the groups are known as stanzas. We sometimes call them verses.

Stream of consciousness

Usually in writing we structure our ideas into an orderly sequence and use sentences and paragraphs to help the reader to follow what we mean. Stream of consciousness means allowing one idea to follow another in an unstructured way. It feels closer to the way we dream than the way we usually write.

Symbolism

We are surrounded by symbols – a green light on a traffic light means go. A plastic poppy in November symbolises the sacrifice of soldiers who took part in the wars. A crucifix symbolises Christian faith. In literature, writers use symbolism to show a layer of meaning beneath the surface. In 'A Case of Murder' (page 86), the black cat at the end of the poem has become more than an ordinary cat.

Syllable

We can break words down into single units of sound. For example, paper has two syllables – pap+er; difficult has three syllables – diff+i+cult. Words of one syllable are described as monosyllabic; words with many syllables are polysyllabic.

Synonyms

Synonyms are words that have similar meanings – for example, closed, shut, locked. The meaning of all of these words is not *exactly* the same: closing a car door is not the same as locking it. But the words are close enough in meaning to allow us to class them as synonyms.

Tone

This describes the writer's voice – whether it is serious, humorous, neutral, sarcastic and so on. The tone of a poem might change as it develops.

Solution to task on page 44

The Fallow Deer at the Lonely House

One without looks in tonight
    Through the curtain-chink
From the sheet of glistening white;
One without looks in tonight
5   As we sit and think
    By the fender-brink.

We do not discern those eyes
    Watching in the snow;
Lit by lamps of rosy dyes
10 We do not discern those eyes
    Wondering, aglow,
    Fourfooted, tiptoe.

Thomas Hardy

Solution to puzzle on page 75

Answers

A = books   **D** = toilet
B = car   **E** = dreams
C = telephone